ADVANCE PRAISE FOR

OPENING THIRD SPACES FOR RESEARCH IN EDUCATION: CHALLENGING THE LIMITS OF TECHNOCRATIC METHODS

"Blakely and Hemphill have written a methods book that our field desperately needs. They have taken to task the profound lack of ingenuity, courage, and challenge to long-standing racist, classist, homophobic, and patriarchal patterns in the field of education and, specifically, education research. This is worth reading for all researchers. It is essential reading for those aiming to develop research practices that disrupt the radicalized inequities in our field."

Jeff Duncan-Andrade, Professor,
Latina/o Studies & Race and Resistance Studies,
San Francisco State University

"This text is one that any equity-minded education faculty teaching a graduate or upper level undergraduate class on research methodology should adopt. Blakley and Hemphill provide a valuable addition to our field by using an orientation rarely even discussed in other methods texts. Third space allows them to investigate intersectional identities and critical theory as it plays out in research design, analysis, and genres of representation. The book is joyfully well researched, crisply written, and brings together topics I often address in my teaching, yet never before with the support of a single text."

Barbara A. Henderson, Director,
Doctoral Program in Educational Leadership
Graduate College of Education,
San Francisco State University

"*Opening Third Spaces for Research in Education: Challenging the Limits of Technocratic Methods* is a remarkable work. Extremely well written and richly rewarding. It contains a brilliant analysis of the problems haunting education today and it develops new ways of thinking and acting when it comes to educational research. A must read for anyone seriously interested in educational research today."

Klaus Nielsen, Professor,
Department of Psychology,
Aarhus University, Denmark

"*Opening Third Spaces for Research in Education: Challenging the Limits of Technocratic Methods* offers a powerful argument for shifting the focus of research away from the overly formalistic concerns with conducting research *correctly* towards research that is aligned with the subject matter in education. The book—spanning the philosophical underpinnings of different research traditions, the ways research as a subject is taught to students, and the concepts researched (e.g., learning)—enlightens the reader regarding the many alternative ways relevant research may be conducted in education. A highly recommended read for everyone planning to do research in education."

Jacob Klitmøller,
Associate Professor of Educational Psychology,
Department of Psychology,
Aarhus University, Denmark

"The brilliance of *Opening Third Spaces for Research in Education: Challenging the Limits of Technocratic Methods* lies in its being situated in colonial historicity that privileged Western psychological research models which have, by and large, colonized educational research under the pretext of protecting objectivity. By succinctly unveiling the falsehood upon which the foundational pillars that support the false binarism inherent in the derivative educational research models, Erin Blakely and David Hemphill, painstakingly demonstrate how the disarticulation between the interpretative discourse and the interests of the interpreter often denies the dialectical relationship between subjectivity and objectivity. That is, the blind embrace of objectivity found in most educational research, denies the subjectivity that determines why a particular area is considered worthy of research in the first place, and how certain knowledges are subordinated to the imperatives of number crunching which, by design, erases the human face always present in all research endeavors.

What the authors of *Opening Third Spaces for Research in Education: Challenging the Limits of Technocratic Methods* make abundantly clear is the high societal costs exacted through the Godfication of scientism, not science, and the blind celebration of methodological elegance. Given the unacceptable high rate of educational failure, particularly in urban areas populated mostly by non-white students, readers of this important book will understand that the predominance of the technocratic paradigm in educational research is an ideological trap that sacrifices human factors along the lines of gender, ethnicity, class, and culture at the altar of research objectivity. This insightful book must be read by all educators who consider themselves agents of change in the struggle to promote a less dystopian and more humane world."

Donaldo Macedo, Ph.D.
Professor Emeritus and Distinguished Professor of Liberal Arts
University of Massachusetts Boston

OPENING THIRD SPACES FOR RESEARCH IN EDUCATION

OPENING THIRD SPACES FOR RESEARCH IN EDUCATION

Challenging the Limits of Technocratic Methods

BY ERIN BLAKELY AND

DAVID HEMPHILL

Myers Education Press

Gorham, Maine

Myers Education Press

Published by Myers Education Press, LLC
P.O. Box 424
Gorham, ME 04038

Myers Education Press is an academic publisher specializing in books, e-books and digital content in the field of education. All of our books are subjected to a rigorous peer review process and produced in compliance with the standards of the Council on Library and Information Resources.

Library of Congress Cataloging-in-Publication Data available from Library of Congress.

13-digit ISBN 978-1-9755-0475-5 (paperback)
13-digit ISBN 978-1-9755-0474-8 (hard cover)
13-digit ISBN 978-1-9755-0476-2 (library networkable e-edition)
13-digit ISBN 978-1-9755-0477-9 (consumer e-edition)

Printed in the United States of America.

All first editions printed on acid-free paper that meets the American National Standards Institute Z39-48standard.

Cover design by Teresa Lagrange

Contents

Dedication

This book is dedicated to my husband, Troy, and my son, Sam, for their constant support and to the doctoral students and professors in Denmark who generously shared their work and time.

— Erin Blakely

This book is dedicated to my wife, Jennifer; my daughters, Lydia and Bizzy; and my late parents, Robert and Elizabeth. It is also dedicated to the multiple generations of students whom I have taught over a career of 45 years.

— David Hemphill

Introduction

RESEARCH IN EDUCATION IS SEVERELY limited by the accepted methods for collecting and analyzing data. There is a widespread assumption in the field that "scientific" methods will yield "best practices," without any recognition of how inappropriate the methods of the hard sciences are for studying education and other social relations. There is little, if any, acknowledgment in education of the long history of critique of science—both in its claims of neutrality and its applications to the social world. This critique exists even within the sciences, as quantum physicists upended 100 years ago the claims of Newtonian physics that reality is stable and can be measured by universal laws. These critiques are ignored every time an educational administrator or policymaker asserts that "research shows X" to justify mandated policies and practices.

Even when educational researchers take a critical stance on scientific methods, they often accept uncritically the binaries reproduced in social science research—objective/subjective, theory/practice, quantitative/qualitative—and their inherent power imbalances. These artificial divisions not only discount many kinds of data and research approaches but also limit the research process itself, from defining what counts as a research question to disseminating findings. To counter these limits, this text advocates opening third spaces between these normative binaries and tacitly accepted scientific methods to expand possibilities for research in education.

Binary logic—and its categorical divisions like primitive/civilized and self/Other—has long been integral to the West's colonial projects. This logic is reflected in the field of education, where educators are expected to help "at-risk" students acquire "academic" language and skills, often at the cost of discarding their own discourses and cultures. Deconstructing binaries is key, argued Grewal and Kaplan (1994), since "models predicated upon binary oppositions cannot move us out of the paradigms of colonial discourse, nor can they provide us with accurate maps of social relations" (p. 9). For educational researchers to move out of colonial paradigms and more fully investigate social relations, they must challenge the dominant scientific framework of research methods.

Research instruction in education favors scientific methods over social approaches, privileging form over content, general over specific, and theory over practice. Educators are trained, for example, in technical procedures for conducting "ethical" research, such as sending out informed consent letters, but not in facilitating collaborative decision-making or other ways of navigating ethical dilemmas in the field. Narratives about specific local practices are excluded in favor of research studies that make abstract, generalizable claims. Throughout the research process, methodological policing by research administrators and ethical review boards forces students and researchers to pay more attention to rigidly construed scientific methods than to complex local contexts, histories, and practices. The strict adherence to approved methodologies is imposed in an effort to generate valid and reliable studies that can be widely applied in the field. This misguided goal perpetuates colonial and inequitable social arrangements.

The goal of opening third spaces for research is not to dispense entirely with science and its attendant binaries as a useful framework but to recognize when they are taken for granted, when they can help explain phenomena, and when they erroneously reduce or reify phenomena. When describing social relations, for instance (Black/White, male/female), binaries are reductive and embedded with hierarchical power relations, and scientific methods—when applied uncritically—simply reproduce inequities. Creating third spaces in between these homogenized categories and methods can enable educators to investigate more fully the complexities that compose learning and social relations.

Third spaces refer to material and discursive locations, as well as processes. As Bhabha (1994) wrote, operating in third spaces allows

> focus on those moments or processes that are produced in the articulation of cultural differences. These "in-between" spaces provide the terrain for elaborating strategies . . . that initiate new signs of identity, and innovative sites of collaboration, contestation, in the act of defining the idea of society itself. . . . The interstitial passage between fixed identifications opens up the possibility of a cultural hybridity that entertains difference without an assumed or imposed hierarchy. (pp. 1–9)

In the border lives of students who move between cultures, for example, the third spaces they occupy are not simply a mixture of two established cultures but hybrid spaces where signs and meanings are appropriated, rehistoricized, and read anew. In third spaces, students can "develop a sense of agency in making flexible cross-cultural identifications and in critiquing the socio-cultural practices . . . a place from which to reflect . . . [and] verbalize the arbitrary nature of the linguistic and cultural norms of the two societies" (Lam, 2004, p. 8).

Situated in a third space between the U.S., Mexican, and Indigenous cultures, Anzaldúa (1999), for example, found that she must constantly

> shift out of habitual formations; from convergent thinking, analytical reasoning that tends to use rationality to move toward a single goal (a Western mode), to divergent thinking, characterized by movement away from set patterns and goals toward a more whole perspective, one that includes rather than excludes. (p. 101)

Third spaces are thus productive sites for reflection (Ayala, 2016; Rosaldo, 1989). They are, Gutiérrez et al. (1999) argued, "a useful lens, a theoretical tool for understanding the inherent diversity and heterogeneity of activity systems and learning events" (p. 288).

To illustrate the potential of third spaces in education, Gutiérrez et al. (1999) explained how a teacher disrupted the binary logic that separates academic discussions from student talk, jokes, or slang. When a student made an "inappropriate" comment during a class reading about the human body—"No wonder they call me bony," Jorge joked when the class was asked to locate their spine—the teacher folded his comment into the class discussion. Rather than treating this comment as an unwelcome disruption and disciplining him, the comment

> becomes part of the classroom text. . . . Jorge . . . reemerges as expert in the official space as he answers the question that the teacher had been so intent on asking. . . . His answer and the teacher's enthusiastic response co-constructs Jorge's identity as a knowing contributor. He is not simply the comical contributor; he is also a resource in the classroom. (Gutiérrez et al., 1999, pp. 299–300)

Contrary to the common assumption that joking with peers during class time is an interruption of the learning process, Rasmussen (2016) showed how such actions are "not necessarily an expression of 'participation in opposition' . . . to school or academic subjects, and cannot be understood in isolation from their participation and engagement in . . . other contexts" (p. 236). The assumption that peer talk is an interruption of learning is based on the taken-for-granted binary that learners are separate from what is to be learned. In third spaces, "no single language . . . is privileged, and the larger linguistic repertoires of participants become tools for participating and making meaning in this new collaborative activity. . . . [T]hese hybrid language practices . . . [can increase] the possibility of dialogue—and thus, interpretation" (Gutiérrez et al., 1999, p. 293).

In opening third spaces for educational research, this text aims not only to challenge scientific truisms and disrupt normative binaries but to expand possibilities for dialogue, interpretation, and action. The goal here is not to present a codified or new approach to research. The book does not prescribe a specific sequence of research practices or methods; it rejects the notion that research techniques of any sort can be applied universally. Rather, the text offers researchers the historical and conceptual background necessary to contextualize current practice and question its underlying assumptions—generally so normalized that they seem neutral or inevitable to educators.

In trying to avoid a narrative of progress, which suggests that new forms of research are inherently better than past forms, this book does not use the term *third space research*, implying that this is a new product—an end in itself. Research is often commodified in this way, turned into a product, codified, and packaged. Instead of advocating for "third space" or any specific new type of research, the text advocates shifting from using research as a noun—a packaged thing—to using it primarily as a verb: a doing. Thus, the book does not teach educators how to conduct "third space research" or write a "third space research" report. What the text does is to help educators see from multiple perspectives and expand their action possibilities for ongoing inquiry in education.

The book draws from scholarship across disciplines—ranging from anthropology to critical psychology to quantum physics—to help educational researchers reconceptualize learning and knowledge in ways that avoid reproducing the status quo and its unequal social arrangements. The book also draws on scholarship from across eras, rejecting the modernist idea that the most recent work is always the most advanced. Numerous past works—texts by pragmatists such as Dewey (1910) or philosophers of science such as Kuhn

(1969) and Popper (1963, 1968)—have more to offer educational researchers than many contemporary discussions of research methods.

While the book rejects the privileging of hard sciences and quantitative research methods, it does not simply move in the "opposite" direction to embrace only qualitative work and subjective experience. The text blurs the artificial division between science and social practice, acknowledging how they overlap and coexist within each other. The argument is not that science is not real or necessary; in an era of climate change and global pandemics, ignoring data threatens the very existence of life. The argument is that science does not stand alone—it is a discourse that is unavoidably entangled with the physical and social worlds. The goal is not to get away from facts but closer to them. This means that instead of pouring educational research resources into national standardized testing and expert external researchers, resources need to be allocated directly to educators for developing and sustaining their own inquiry practices. This requires far more than a single methods course. Instead of offering a one-time course in how to design studies that can yield universal "best practices," the aim of opening third spaces for research is to expand approaches and opportunities for ongoing inquiry that directly support educators and their communities.

References

Anzaldúa, G. (1999). *Borderlands/La frontera: The new Mestiza*. Aunt Lute Press.

Ayala, J. (2016). Split scenes, converging visions: The ethical terrains where PAR and borderlands scholarship meet. In P. H. Hinchey (Ed.), *A critical action research reader* (pp. 199–210). Peter Lang.

Bhabha, H. K. (1994). *The location of culture*. Routledge.

Dewey, J. (1910). *How we think*. Cosimo Classics.

Grewal, I., & Kaplan, C. (Eds.). (1994). *Scattered hegemonies: Postmodernity and transnational feminist practices*. University of Minnesota Press.

Gutiérrez, K. D., Baquedano-López, P., & Tejeda, C. (1999). Rethinking diversity: Hybridity and hybrid language practices in the third space. *Mind, Culture, and Activity, 6*(4), 286–303.

Kuhn, T. S. (1969). *The structure of scientific revolutions*. University of Chicago Press.

Lam, W. S. E. (2004). Border discourses and identities in transnational youth culture. In J. Mahiri (Ed.), *What they don't learn in school: Literacy in the lives of urban youth* (pp. 79–98). Peter Lang.

Popper, K. (1963). *Conjectures and refutations: The growth of scientific knowledge*. Routledge.

Popper, K. (1968). *The logic of scientific discovery*. Harper & Row.

Rasmussen, M. S. (2016). Learning from a social practice theoretical perspective. In A. Qvortrup, M. Wiberg, G. Christensen, & M. Hansbøl (Eds.), *On the definition of learning* (pp. 229–244). University Press of Southern Denmark.

Rosaldo, R. (1989). *Culture and truth: The remaking of social analysis*. Beacon Press.

ONE

Examining Scientism in Educational Research

EDUCATION, ALONG WITH ANTHROPOLOGY, PSYCHOLOGY, and other social science fields, is often relegated to a pseudoscience status, undervalued in comparison to the "hard sciences" such as physics, chemistry, and biology. Social scientists have responded to this perception in part by adopting what they believe are rigorous scientific methods for designing and conducting research. This reflects the discourse of **scientism**—the belief that Western science is the sole approach through which the growth of knowledge can be legitimized and disseminated. Accordingly, research methods courses, institutional review boards, university requirements, and national funding stipulations all maintain a preference for quantitatively based control group studies. The aim is to generate valid and reliable educational theory and best practices that can be applied across the field.

The phrase *research shows* is ubiquitous in education, heard in conference halls, university classrooms, district offices, principals' offices, staff lunchrooms, parent conferences, and professional development meetings. It is used regularly in schools to justify all manner of conflicting educational practices from literacy instruction to parent engagement strategies. Though the idea that scientific research should inform practice may seem incontrovertible, this view is itself an historical artifact of the larger, problematic modernist project of the Western Enlightenment. Although many scholars outside the field of education have challenged the objectivity and privileging of scientific knowledge, such critical scholarship—philosophies of science, pragmatism, phenomenology, critical theory, postmodernism, and agential realism—has been ignored or treated reductively in the field of education. Applying this critical scholarship to educational research can help open up third spaces for inquiry.

1.1 Technocratic research and the commodification of knowledge.

Educational researchers rely almost without exception on technical means and expertise, including testing, psychometrics, econometrics, and other quantitative measures to identify best practices. The search for evidence-based best practices reflects a larger **technocratic** project—the attempt to control outcomes by means of technology implemented via an elite of technical experts. As Mehta (2013) observed, multiple U.S. educational reforms over the past century involved the imposition of technocratic logic on the educational sphere. He pointed out that over the course of the 20th century, there were three major movements demanding accountability in American education: the efficiency reforms of the Progressive Era at the turn of the 20th century; a largely forgotten movement toward accountability in the late 1960s and early 1970s; and the modern standards and accountability movement, culminating in No Child Left Behind (NCLB) and the Common Core State Standards of the early 21st century. In each case, Mehta wrote, this process exhibits a similar pattern:

> 1) the creation of a crisis of quality which destabilized the existing educational status quo; 2) the elevation of a technocratic logic, backed by the knowledge base of a high status epistemic community; 3) the rallying of ideologically diverse powerful actors external to the schools behind a commensurating logic that promised control and improvement over an unwieldy school system; and 4) the inability of the education field to resist (and often to be co-opted by) this technocratic logic, due to its historical institutionalization as a highly feminized, weak, bureaucratically administered field lacking its own set of widely respected countervailing professional standards. (p. 1)

In the field of education, learning itself is defined in technocratic terms. As Kvale (1976) wrote, "Learning is the molding of human raw material by the most effective means to some externally defined end . . . where the goals are taken as given and the problem is to find the most effective means of reaching the goal" (p. 107). The technical effectivizing of education has been adopted by the U.S. Department of Education (2019) as the mission statement for its research arm:

> The mission of the Institute of Education Sciences (IES) is to provide rigorous and relevant evidence on which to ground education practice and policy and share this information broadly. By identifying what works, what doesn't, and why, IES aims to improve educational outcomes for all students, particularly those at risk of failure.

In this technocratic landscape, teachers are trained in formulaic, research-based practices rather than, for example, the historical role or critical social context of schooling. Most professional development time is spent on abstract topics, examining how techniques, devices, or curriculum can improve specific learning outcomes. A typical goal of a grade-level meeting may be, for instance, to measure which techniques work best to improve reading fluency rates, or which classroom management strategies improve time on task. Teachers are also quantitatively evaluated based on how well their students perform on standardized assessment measures. The drive to rank and evaluate teachers and school systems accompanies the proliferation of high-stakes testing regimes.

The resulting narrow parameters that constrain educators produce a normative developmental model that leads to a rigid system of measurement, where learning is understood only through behavioral quantification. Children are tracked throughout their schooling and identified and ranked by their literacy and math levels. Publishing and testing corporations and researchers quantify student performances to distill, package, and market them as commodities. Most schools from PreK to university must now deliver "student learning outcomes"—specific, measurable products for all disciplines.

Educational policies support and embody the **commodification** of knowledge—turning it into a product that can be measured, bought, and sold. Marx (1887/1971) defined a commodity as "an object outside us, a thing that by its properties satisfies human wants of some sort or another" (p. 48). Commodification of most aspects of life is characteristic of a globalized era where relations of social belonging are steeped in consumption of physical, symbolic, and virtual products. Consumption is a coded system of signs through which people communicate with one another, and it extends beyond purchasing a product to the entire range of symbolic uses of products, knowledge, services, technologies, and people (Baudrillard, 1988).

In addition to quantifying student skills, commodification in schools reifies knowledge as an objective domain that is separate from students, teachers, and the learning process. School curriculum and assessments artificially separate social practices, decontextualizing and then assessing them on an abstract continuum. Universal screening measures reinforce this division, providing assessment data on an array of presumably discrete skills. Standardized measurement systems erroneously normalize the idea that context is irrelevant—that student learning is untouched by passage of time, topic selection, test-taking environment, teacher–student relationship, affective conditions, or community norms. Teachers commodify and assess students' literacy skills, for example, by asking them to read aloud from a leveled passage. Students are then informed of their "lexile" or "grade-level score" and directed to particular texts, which are color coded or sorted by level. These literacy tests ignore contextual factors and assume that students have the same reading level at all times, regardless of topic or social and material conditions.

The commodification of knowledge in schools is one dimension of the larger commodification of knowledge in contemporary society. As Hussey and Smith (2002) claimed, "Education has become a commodity, and the 'products' it offers to its 'customers' have had to be commodified: divided into distinct, measurable quantities or modules each capable of being 'bought' by prescribed units of assessment" (p. 220). Education has, Apple (1998) argued further, "become a marketable commodity like bread and cars in which the values, procedures, and metaphors of business dominate" (p. 25). Schools are monitored, audited, and evaluated so that results can be measured and compared. In this outputs-driven context, Lave and McDermott (2002) argued, the learners produce not for themselves but for their place in the system.

In the drive toward market-like efficiency, educators are tasked with discriminating between ever finer grained skills, improving their distribution, and maximizing learning outcomes. As Lyotard (1999) wrote, the important distinction is "no longer . . . between ignorance and knowledge, but rather . . . between . . . units of knowledge exchanged in a daily maintenance framework ['payment knowledge'] . . . versus funds of knowledge dedicated to optimizing the performance of a project ['investment knowledge']" (p. 7). For such an exchange system to take place, there must be a precise system of measurement and accountability, as schools have become part of an outputs-driven performance culture. This focus on observing and measuring knowledge products has led to standardization of curricula and school programming so that students receive the same amount of instruction on the same age-graded schedule. It is common practice to calculate university rankings, school or district performance indicators, Academic Performance Index scores, and other quantifiable measures of learning outcomes. All of these commodify knowledge in schools.

The increasing dominance of **neoliberal** economic policies in the late 20th and early 21st centuries further pushed educational policy, research, and practice in what is claimed to be a scientific direction. Neoliberal economic policies began to hold sway in the United States, Great Britain, and other countries starting in the early 1980s when President Ronald Reagan and Prime Minister Margaret Thatcher promoted sweeping changes in national and international economic rhetoric and policy. International institutions like the World Bank and the International Monetary Fund were the vanguard of this impetus. The results systematically altered public policy on a global scale in an approach referred to as "neoliberal economics" or the "Washington Consensus." As Klees (2008) recounted, neoliberal economic policies call for a series of interrelated government-wide reforms, including

- maintaining macroeconomic stability,
- cutting back government budgets,
- privatizing government operations,
- ending tariffs and other forms of protection,
- facilitating movement of foreign capital,
- emphasizing exports,
- charging user fees for many public services, and
- reducing worker protections through flexible labor markets.

In the field of education, neoliberal thinking had particular impact in three areas: tying management and financing of education to measurable output, cost recovery and increased use of user fees, and privatization of educational activities. The first area—the focus on assessing measurable output—has had the greatest influence on educational research. The emphasis on assessment led to an increase in teaching to the test, narrowing curriculum to the extent that subjects not covered on standardized tests receive little or no instructional time. Teacher merit pay, too, is often tied to test results.

In this neoliberal landscape, educators rely heavily on the notion that standardized measures of student success permit comparisons across techniques and settings, including teachers, grade levels, schools, districts, regions, and nations. This has further contributed to a drive for standardized instruction, since it is assumed that when students have a uniform schooling experience, they can be more easily studied, sorted, and ranked.

The reliance on standardized assessments has many consequences, such as the underestimation of student potential. Students mistakenly assessed as "below basic" on a single-leveled text may actually be able to decode texts of different genres—such as high-interest nonfiction texts, fan fiction, or technical gaming instructions. Measures that label these students as "at risk," "below grade level," or "emerging reader" can unnecessarily limit access to grade-level texts and curriculum resources. In this way, students are produced as commodities of failure. McDermott (1996) argued that when young people are labeled as "learning disabled," they have actually been "acquired" as commodities by the category of their labeling:

> [Learning disabled] exists as a category in our culture, and it will acquire a certain proportion of our children as long as it is given life in the organization of tasks, skills, and evaluations in our schools. . . . The labels precede any child's entry into the world . . . and stand poised to take their share from each new generation. (pp. 271–272)

Commodification of learners is widespread in Western education, as students are regularly trapped into categories in ways that are difficult to breach.

The neoliberal commodification of knowledge exists at the highest institutional levels. The U.S. National Reading Panel (NRP) provides one example. First implemented during the NCLB era, NRP illustrates the bias within the U.S. Department of Education in favor of technocratic research focused narrowly on experimentally derived causal explanations of program effectiveness. Beginning in the late 1990s, the NRP was formed to "bring order" to the field of reading research knowledge:

> The Panel . . . developed and adopted a set of rigorous research methodological standards . . . [to contribute to] a better scientific understanding of reading development and reading instruction. . . . The evidence ultimately evaluated by

> the Panel met well-established objective scientific standards. . . . [Studies were disqualified] if they were not reporting experimental or quasi experimental studies, if they were not published in English, or if they dealt exclusively with learning disabled or other special populations, including second language learners. (National Institute of Child Health and Human Development, 2000, pp. 5–27)

Circumscribed notions of scientifically based research were used not only to narrow literacy practices but also to limit the professional discretion of teachers. Curriculum mandates, pacing guides, and test-driven curricula shifted the focus in professional development and teacher evaluation toward fidelity to research-based practices. Though claiming neutrality, the technocratic discourse of NCLB was neither value-free nor objective. As Pearson (2004) argued, it was part of a larger agenda of centralized control and deskilling teachers:

> For the past 30 years, a conservative lobby has been trying to manipulate several policy levers (standards, assessment, professional development, and evidence-based practice) to shape a national reading policy that privileges basic skills for students and limits teacher education to training rather than educative practices. [It] . . . could be characterized as a sort of 'skill the kids and de-skill the teachers' approach. (p. 231)

Eight years after the NRP was initiated, government researchers found that the percentage of students actually engaged with print, both fiction and nonfiction, had declined. Students using a research-based approach were no better than before at drawing meaning from texts, according to the government's own research (Sparks, 2012). Despite continuing research, literacy debates have yet to be resolved (Pearson, 2004; Purcell-Gates et al., 2007). Yet a technocratic emphasis on quantitative, experimental methods remains the focus of government-supported educational research. As Kvale (1976) concluded, "Although the traditional theories of learning have not led to direct improvements of learning, they have functioned ideologically as a scientific legitimation of a technological education practice" (p. 110).

The initiation of the Common Core State Standards (CCSS) in the United States in 2010 was advertised as a corrective to the problems of NCLB.

Through CCSS, "education bureaucrats . . . nationalized public school curriculum and assessment in language arts and mathematics through the adoption of a universal set of core curriculum standards and a national standardized testing program" (Tienkin, 2013, p. 310). Yet CCSS has continued to narrow curriculum and deskill teachers: "Many districts have implemented CCSS in a way that "rob[s] teachers of professional agency by scripting curriculum, marginalizing teachers from the decision-making process, and adding to the risk-reward imbalance created by the state" (Endacott et al., 2015, p. 433). The CCSS and its accompanying "Smarter Balanced" assessment system simply extends NCLB while continuing to commodify student learning into measurable units for comparison across districts and regions.

Educational administrators and policymakers have expanded the use of standardized test results to make life-influencing decisions about children, teachers, and schooling while opportunities shrink for "low-performing" students placed in reductionist academic tracks. Yet proponents of CCSS exhort parents and teachers to embrace the neoliberal project of commodification of knowledge to help students compete in the global economy: "With American students fully prepared for the future, our communities will be best positioned to compete successfully in the global economy" (Common Core State Standards Initiative, n.d.). Advocates of this market-based, competitive vision of schooling move school practice further away from democratic citizenship toward commodified economic citizenship. Educational research has for too long served the interests of neoliberal projects that maintain inequities for the flawed purpose of promoting scientific rigor.

1.2 The dominance of positivism and behaviorism.

Since education became an object of scientific inquiry in the emergent field of psychology at the end of the 1800s, educators have been told persistently that scientific research should inform their practice. Despite decades of critique, much of contemporary educational research remains closely fixed to a scientistic theoretical position. The prevailing technocratic paradigm in educational research is promoted ahistorically as the inevitable and only valid form of inquiry.

Western science from the 17th century onward has been valorized in most parts of the world as the sole, legitimate source of knowledge. Over time, scholars have formalized its methods so that research instruction now has nearly identical content in higher education throughout the world. Few, if any, other research approaches have been afforded space to emerge globally because of the domination of Western English-speaking research institutions, universities, and publications.

Most, if not all, university research methods courses present a linear research process with prescribed methods for each stage. These procedures are deemed so crucial for legitimizing research that researchers and students spend far more time on methods than on the history, context, or implications of their investigations. Research methods instruction in education generally neglects the histories of science and social science research, taking for granted that scientific research advances ever upward toward improved knowledge. Yet the history of science has always been a contested domain despite how the field of education has reduced it to a technocratic project that makes universal claims.

The Western scientific method is actually an **ethnoscience**—one of many culturally based scientific approaches (Harding, 1998). Other ethnosciences—for instance, those of China, the Islamic World, and South Asia—were developed prior to Western science and influenced its content, while reflecting their own social and historical contexts (Needham, 1954; Nelson et al., 1993). The aim of Western science—to make predictions and control phenomena in the physical world—is not shared by all other ethnosciences. Though Western scientific methods may be well suited to the expansive aims of technology development, biomedical innovation, and industrialization, they are rarely suited to the social and educational disciplines that have unquestioningly adopted its methods.

Early Western science emerged in the work of Bacon in Europe in the 16th century. His inductive approach elevated experiment and observation over reason, intuition, and convention. Induction involves collecting facts through direct experience and arranging them into theories. The inductive model was intended as a corrective to the earlier classical Greek subordination of inquiry to Aristotelian intuitions, and as a condemnation of appeals to political-religious dogmas influential in Europe prior to the Enlightenment (Harris, 1979).

Bacon was opposed by many, including Descartes, who searched for certainty through deduction. There were thus two camps: the Empiricists and Positivists (Bacon's view) versus the Cartesians and Rationalists (Descartes's view). Yet, in the actual work of the sciences, neither type of thought was pursued exclusively. Western science became an innovative interplay between induction and deduction in which the investigator first operates inductively from observations to hypotheses; then operates deductively from these hypotheses to their implications, in order to check their validity from the standpoint of compatibility with accepted knowledge; then, after revision as needed, submits hypotheses to further tests and inductive analysis through the collection of data specifically designed to test their validity at the empirical level; and finally links together new findings with prior findings, again employing deductive reasoning.

In the 17th and 18th centuries, the inductive/deductive scientific method was codified and became a key element of modernism that has dominated Western thought ever since. The main tenets of modernism are so thoroughly embedded in the conceptual frameworks, languages, and socioeconomic systems of the West that they seem natural, inevitable, and universal, though they are rarely stated or discussed. Primary elements of **modernism** include

- a privileging of logic, rationality, and observable evidence as the most reliable, legitimate paths to truth and knowledge;
- an emphasis on overarching **metanarratives**—theories that seek to explain everything, like the narrative of progress that organizes history in an ever-upward march toward advanced civilization;
- a reliance on form over content—for example, emphasizing process in legal proceedings or methods in research training;
- a tendency to see things as binaries (either/or), such as mind/body, rational/irrational, science/humanities, male/female, White/Black, or self/Other; and
- a conceptualization of subjectivity that defines the individual as being of primary importance, and characterizes the "normal" adult self as rational, stable, autonomous, fully transparent to itself, and responsible for its actions. (Hemphill & Blakely, 2015, p. 2)

The application of the methods of modernist science to the social world was advanced through Comte's **positivism** in the early 19th century. Comte, who was the first philosopher of science in the modern sense, claimed that a new age of science was dawning. He termed this new emergence *positivistic* because he assumed that science should now be based on well-tested, systematized, positive knowledge validated through observation and measurement. Comte established four basic rules of positivism to define valid scientific inquiry—and thus all conceivable systematic inquiry and knowledge production about the social world:

1. All knowledge must be proven through the "sense certainty" of systematic observation. It is only sense experience that can provide access to the domain of facts and truth.
2. Methodological certainty must be guaranteed by adherence to a rigid set of procedures.
3. Facts must be connected to theories, which are constructed in a form that permits the deduction of lawlike hypotheses.
4. Scientific findings must also be practical and technically usable. (Habermas, 1971)

Under the influence of positivism, independent observers become the line between science and other forms of knowledge through the formulation of testable hypotheses whose truth depends upon observations or experiments. By testing hypotheses and accepting some as better confirmed than others, science is seen to advance in linear fashion toward ever more powerful and accurate theories, from which predictions about an increasingly wide range of phenomena can be made.

Through positivism Comte sought to establish a foundation for social inquiry or sociology, then called *social physics*. He asserted that valid knowledge or truth about any phenomenon—physical or social—can be derived only through direct empirical observation and verification via scientific methods, by using logical and mathematical analyses to describe and explain experience. Comte explicitly rejected centuries of philosophical argument, which posited a difference between natural philosophy and moral philosophy. According to Comte, this distinction, introduced by the Greeks, was abolished by the existence of positivist social inquiry.

For Comte, method is superior to doctrine: Scientific doctrines change (that is what progress means to Comte), but the value of science is argued to lie in its unchanging methods. Positivism, accordingly, is concerned with the degree to which any phenomena can be precisely measured and determined.

Since Comte maintained that science must be proven through "sense certainty" and grounded in careful, systematic procedures, positivism ultimately "asserts the priority of method over substance" (Habermas, 1971, p. 75). This approach presumes that research methods can be made pure, unbiased, and free of taints that might color data collection and analysis. The approach further denies the existence of phenomena beyond the immediately observable. This produces a narrowly behaviorist social science that fixates on quantitative measurement of observable phenomena.

Positivism also led to the belief that all scientific inquiry should result in the technical control of natural and social processes. As Comte asserted, "All of our sound theories [are necessarily related] to the continuous improvement of our individual and collective conditions of life" (as cited in Habermas, 1971, p. 76). This requirement means that for findings to be considered valid, they must fit into existing universalizable metanarratives. It also means that findings that do not fit into established structures are ignored or rejected as anomalies. Positivists accordingly seek to impose underlying causal or theoretical connections onto all facts. These connections are meant to transcend "mere description" to yield broad generalizations, even if no such connections are actually found in the data.

Positivists believe, too, that uncertainty or questions of morality or ethics are not expected to arise if Comte's four rules are followed. If the form of the scientific method is carefully followed, positivists assume that the findings will be objectively derived and irrefutable. Their system of knowledge is thus constructed as a closed loop, as scientists believe they have no reason to call their methods or logic into question.

Subsequent developments in positivistic thinking took place in the first half of the 20th century, initially in Europe and subsequently in the United States. This new iteration of positivism came to be called *logical positivism* or *logical empiricism*. According to logical positivists, there are only two sources of knowledge: logical reasoning and empirical observation. The ultimate basis of all knowledge is said to rest upon observable experimental verification rather than upon personal or social experience. Further, logical positivists believe that the only meaningful problems are those that can be solved by logical analysis. Problems that cannot be addressed in this way are rejected as unworthy of formal investigation.

The behaviorist movement in psychology, led in the 20th century by Watson (1913) and Skinner (1957), extrapolates on the claims of logical positivism. **Behaviorism** emphasizes the role of environmental factors in influencing human actions, to the near exclusion of biological, mental, or inherited factors. Skinner and Watson declared that concepts such as mind, intuition, instinct, and meaning are all metaphysical survivals, unworthy of study because they cannot be empirically observed, operationally defined, or satisfactorily measured (Watson, 1913). Though behaviorists may accept in a limited way the existence of cognition and emotions, they prefer not to study them, as they believe that only observable external behavior can be objectively and scientifically measured. Therefore, behaviorists believe that internal events, such as thinking and feeling, can be explained only through externally observable and measurable behavioral indicators—or simply ignored altogether.

In the early 20th century, Bridgman (1927) contributed the concept of operationalization to behaviorist research. **Operationalization** is the practice of defining research variables solely in terms of their measurement methods, and in ways that are repeatable by anyone: "The proper definition of a concept is not in terms of its properties, but in terms of actual operations," and thus a concept is "nothing more than a set of operations" (Bridgman, as cited in Russell, 1928, p. 355). This means that all key variables in a technocratic research study require an "operational definition." For example, a researcher may wish to operationalize—and thus to measure—the concept of anger. From a behaviorist perspective, the presence of anger and the depth of the emotion cannot be measured directly by an outside observer, because anger is seen as intangible. Rather, observable indicators claimed to represent anger are identified and measured via such phenomena as facial expression, choice of vocabulary, or loudness and tone of voice.

Through operationalization Bridgman formalized and advanced the views of positivists and behaviorists by claiming that the phenomena being studied are literally identical to the methods used—that methodological form is indistinguishable from research content. This is widely accepted in educational research, yet many other scholars challenge this claim:

> If operations literally *define* concepts (i.e., the concept is *nothing but* the operation by which it is defined), then each operation defines a new concept. For instance, length-as-measured-by-ruler, length-as-measured-by triangulation,

> and length-as-measured-by radar become entirely distinct concepts—in every way as independent as are, say, length and mass. (Green, 2001, p. 46)

Challenged as early as 1928, the year after Bridgman published his first piece on the subject, operationalism remains a contested question in psychology, the field of its origin (Russell, 1928). As Green (2001) asserted, "The primary difficulty with operationism . . . was that it was proposed as a solution to a metaphysical problem that it was not even remotely adequate to meet" (p. 45).

A firm rebuttal of behaviorism came with Chomsky's (1975) review of Skinner's (1957) book *Verbal Behavior*. Chomsky showed that by insisting on fixed procedures appropriate to the study of rats, Skinner obscured the most distinctive aspect of human language: an intuited sense of what is grammatical. Chomsky's critique was a turning point in a theoretical shift from behaviorism toward **cognitivism** in psychology—a movement developed in response to behaviorism's exclusive focus on external behaviors. It focused instead on internal cognitive functions (information processing, attention, memory, thinking).

Cognitivism and related neuroscience research were co-opted, however, by the behaviorist discourses of technocratic research. For instance, it is common in the field of education to hear educators discuss cognitivist concepts such as multiple intelligences, distributed cognition, or metacognition while still applying a behavioristic research paradigm that references student learning outcomes, high-stakes testing, and other performance-based or external measures of learning.

Logical positivists hold that scientific knowledge is the only kind of factual knowledge and that all "metaphysical" doctrines—abstract concepts such as being, knowing, identity, or God—should be rejected. They argue that metaphysical questions are not false but simply meaningless because they are "not genuine questions" at all. This view is reflected in research methods courses when professors tell students that the research questions they pose are "not researchable" or they are "unanswerable" because they cannot be operationalized quantitatively, and thus do not adhere to the technocratic measurement frameworks of Western science.

Logical positivists further claim that a statement is meaningful only if it can be proved true or false, at least in principle. This assertion is called the verifiability principle. According to Ayer (1936),

> We say that a sentence is factually significant to any given person, if and only if, he knows how to verify the proposition which it purports to express—that is, if he knows what observations would lead him, under certain conditions, to accept the proposition as being true, or reject it as being false. (p. 16)

The verifiability principle significantly limits the scope of possible investigations. Yet Popper (1963) argued that the verifiability principle is unattainable. He asserted that knowledge cannot be verified and must always remain conjectural and revisable. Therefore, science cannot offer a consistent method for verifying hypotheses. Though scientists may initially be motivated to conduct observations to further their understanding of a phenomenon, in practice their observations are often treated reductively and deployed as "proof" to justify policies.

The best that science can do, Popper argued, is to falsify a hypothesis. For instance, the hypothesis "All swans are white" cannot be verified even if a million observations have been made of white swans because on the millionth-and-first time, a black swan may still be found. On the other hand, if the hypothesis is restated in a way that falsifies the initial hypothesis—"Not all swans are white"—then, Popper (1963) claimed , knowledge remains conjectural, and no observation of a black swan suffices to reject the negatively stated hypotheses, and thus to confirm the original hypothesis. Popper, in his **falsification** argument, concluded that scientists can only detect and eliminate erroneous theories and inaccurate findings; they can never confirm whether a proposition is true.

To operationalize Popper's assertion, researchers developed the **null hypothesis**. It employs reverse logic, codifying the use of a negated version of the original hypothesis. For instance, if the actual hypothesis of a study is "There is a relationship between age and mathematical ability," then the null hypothesis becomes "Age has no impact on mathematical ability." Positivist researchers believe that if they can find evidence to reject the null hypothesis, then there is a logical basis to claim a potential relationship between the two variables of age and mathematical ability. The null hypothesis is not always stated in research reports, though its existence is generally implied. A common criticism of the null hypothesis is that it is almost always literally false, so "disproving it is both unimpressive and uninformative" (Levine et al., 2008, p. 176). Yet educational researchers continue to employ the null hypothesis, and professors continue to teach it and require its use.

1.3 Scientific paradigm shifts as social consensus.

Despite the widespread notion in education that fidelity to technocratic methods leads to objective knowledge, the practice of science is often different from its idealized characterization:

> Real scientists in their daily work are anything but disinterested and canonically rational. In their daily practice they are passionate and argumentative, profoundly selective in their attention to evidence, and aesthetic in drawing conclusions from it. . . . The actual "culture of science," in other words, is far from the white coat image that appears to the layperson. The accumulation of knowledge in actual science is not at all continuous—it moves by fits and starts. (Erickson & Gutierrez, 2002, p. 22)

A range of scholars in the field of the philosophy of science critique the idealized rationality of science. The philosophy of science emerged as a distinct discipline in the 20th century, calling into question the logical positivist claim that all knowledge should be verified empirically. Philosophers of science explore what qualifies as science, the reliability of scientific theories, and the ultimate purpose of science (Barad, 2007; Feyerabend, 1975; Haraway, 2004; Harding, 1998; Kuhn, 1969; Popper, 1963). It is a broad field, and there is little consensus among philosophers of science about many of the central problems of science, including whether science can reveal the truth about unobservable things, whether there is a measure or algorithm for scientific progress, and whether scientific reasoning can be justified at all. These debates are absent from educational research instruction.

Kuhn (1969) challenged the modernist vision that new research continually advances knowledge in a linear sequence of logically related steps. He rejected the view that later science always builds on the knowledge contained within earlier theories, as well as the developmental view that later theories are closer approximations of truth than prior theories. He argued instead that the process of arriving at new scientific discoveries is often convoluted and disruptive. The development of a science is not uniform, Kuhn observed, but has alternating "normal" and "revolutionary" phases. These phases represent sharp breaks between agreed-upon knowledge frameworks.

Science operates, said Kuhn (1969), within an overarching framework of knowledge called a **paradigm**. A paradigm embodies all scientific knowledge and practice conducted during a particular period of history. Kuhn argued that the world is experienced and investigated according to the principles of the given historical epoch in which it exists. Paradigms thus represent the social consensus among a community of scientists at a given point in time, reflecting prevailing sociohistorical beliefs and constructs. However, scientists generally ignore this social and cultural context or consider it irrelevant.

Paradigms are an unquestioned part of the landscape within which scientists operate. They appear to be static and universal, and they permit no reflection on the historical and social contexts that surround and might challenge them. As Harding (1998) explained, "The problem . . . is that it permits no procedures for identifying those social values and interests that belong to the entire scientific community" (p. 316). The accepted paradigm of any era sets limits on what questions might reasonably be asked and determines the scope of possible research.

Social scientists have rigid expectations for determining a legitimate or researchable question, and these researchable questions, said Kuhn (1969), "are the only problems that the community will admit as scientific or encourage its members to undertake" (p. 37). A paradigm is accompanied by the tendency to choose only those research problems that seem to have solutions that fit within the paradigm.

> Other problems . . . are rejected as metaphysical, as the concern of another discipline, or sometimes as just too problematic to be worth the time. A paradigm can, for that matter, even insulate the community from those socially important problems that are not reducible to the puzzle [researchable] form, because they cannot be stated in terms of the conceptual and instrumental tools the paradigm supplies. (Kuhn, 1969, p. 37)

The current technocratic paradigm in educational research means that the only accepted researchable questions are those framed in behavioral terms that can be operationalized.

Kuhn used the term **normal science** to describe the typical puzzle-solving investigations that occur during the period of dominance of any given paradigm for as long as the existing social consensus on the paradigm holds. Long periods of normal science conducted under a status quo, claimed Kuhn, are interrupted by the buildup of anomalies or research results that do not fit the existing paradigm. Anomalies are generally ignored at first or explained away, if at all possible. The activity of normal science, Kuhn (1969) argued, is

> an attempt to force nature into the preformed and relatively inflexible box that the paradigm supplies. Nor do scientists normally aim to invent new theories, and they are often intolerant of those invented by others. . . . To desert the paradigm is to cease practicing the science it defines. (pp. 24, 34)

Scientists change their minds and paradigms only with great reluctance.

The accumulation of anomalies may at some point pose a serious problem for the existing paradigm, undermining the practice of normal science or revealing inadequacies in commonly used theories. If normal science relies upon this paradigm, then scientists will find it difficult to continue with confidence until the anomalies are addressed. A widespread failure in such confidence Kuhn (1969) called a "crisis." In such a situation, "the rules of normal science become increasingly blurred. Though there still is a paradigm, few practitioners may prove to be entirely agreed about what it is. Even formerly standard solutions of solved problems are then called into question" (p. 83). Ultimately the paradigm shifts to a new shared understanding, which shapes, in its own new terms, the investigations going forward.

A paradigm shift is not, Kuhn (1969) argued, gradual or orderly; it is a revolution in which conceptual apparatuses, experimental methods, and criteria for accuracy change. The rejection of an existing paradigm leads directly to adoption of a new paradigm; as Kuhn wrote, "To reject one paradigm without simultaneously substituting another is to reject science itself" (p. 79).

Paradigm shifts open up new approaches to understandings that scientists would never have considered valid before. Universal scientific truths, then, cannot be established solely by unchanging objective criteria but are instead defined by the shifting sociocultural consensus of scientific communities: "There is no standard higher than the assent of the relevant community. . . . Paradigm choice can never be unequivocally settled by logic and experiment alone" (Kuhn, 1969, p. 94). Truth is therefore culturally mediated and chronologically limited, argued Kuhn, and specific to its own paradigm. Progress in science derives from consensual social agreements among scientists, and scientific truth is determined by social consensus at any specific point in time. The search for knowledge through the scientific method can never rely on full, timeless objectivity. Yet technocratic researchers act as if there are no alternatives to the prevailing paradigm, and they erroneously assume that their paradigm is a product of complete and timeless objectivity.

1.4 Phenomenology of the social world.

Philosophers of science such as Popper (1963, 1968) and Kuhn (1969) are not alone in questioning logical positivism. There is also the movement of **phenomenology**, initially developed by Husserl (1960) in the early 1900s, which studies the ways that individuals experience phenomena. Phenomenological researchers study experience as seen from a subjective, first-person point of view.

A related approach called *social phenomenology* examines how everyday reality is characterized by **intersubjectivity**—the existence of multiple realities among people and their dialogical interaction. When two individuals talk, for example, each brings a different set of experiences and expectations to the encounter, co-constructing their realities. As Berger and Luckmann (1966) put it, reality is socially constructed through "everyday life . . . shared with others" (p. 43).

Intersubjective understanding takes place via empathy, without one person reducing the other to an inanimate physical object or a mathematical expression, as is done in scientific research. Social phenomenologists assert that people give meaning to their social worlds through mirror-like reflections of one another's nature. People and groups interact in a social system to create, over time, shared mental representations of each other's actions, and these concepts eventually become codified as reality in the roles played in relation to each other. When these roles are played out, knowledge and practices are institutionalized. In the process, meaning is embedded in social relations, what Berger and Luckmann (1966) called the **social stock of knowledge**—customs, common interpretations, institutions, shared routines, and social division of labor.

The social stock of knowledge constitutes a much larger part of knowledge in society than what can be captured quantitatively through a narrow technocratic paradigm. As Schutz (1954) stated, positivist researchers created a kind of research monopoly, where "the methods of the [natural sciences] were frequently declared to be the only scientific ones and the particular problems which social scientists encountered in their work were disregarded" (p. 258). Social phenomenologists argue that while the natural sciences have to deal with material objects and processes, the social sciences address psychological and intellectual phenomena. Social phenomenologists assert that the social sciences cannot conform to the logic of the natural sciences (Gadamer, 1976; Habermas, 1971). They suggest that the social sciences should try to understand social action—and not simply build narrow scientistic explanations based on general laws. In a phenomenological approach, researchers do not rely on observation and explanation alone, but instead examine the complex meanings of social practices (Apel, 1984).

In their acceptance of the technocratic paradigm, educational researchers assume that knowledge is an individual's acquisition of information and skills, ignoring how knowledge is socially constructed. Yet every aspect of experience and knowledge construction, Schutz (1954) argued, is characterized by intersubjectivity. Social reality, he asserted, is

> the sum total of objects and occurrences within the social cultural world as experienced by the common-sense thinking of [humans] living their daily lives among their fellow [humans]. . . . It is the interchange of thoughts and feelings, both conscious and unconscious, between two persons or "subjects," as facilitated by empathy. (p. 267)

What is "real" for people does not exist outside of them in some abstract place. Rather, social reality is directly negotiated through dialogue and codified through regular daily practices. There is no separate reality outside of experience, as scientistic researchers assume. The institutionalization of social processes grows out of habits and customs, achieved through mutual agreement on "ways of doing things." This means, for instance, that what students learn in a classroom depends not just upon information a teacher presents but also upon how that information is shared and interpreted among students, prior practices in the classroom, and the physical space itself. Phenomenologists argue that knowledge construction is a shared, intersubjective process. Therefore, it cannot be effectively investigated solely via technocratic methods. Instead, investigations of social action have to reflect the intersubjective experience by adopting methods that accommodate complexity, constant change, and multiple points of view.

Merleau-Ponty (1962) argued that direct, intersubjective experience is primary, whereas science is secondary and derivative:

> The whole universe of science is built upon the world as directly experienced, and if we want to subject science itself to rigorous scrutiny and arrive at a precise assessment of its meaning and scope, we must begin by reawakening the basic experience of the world of which science is the second-order expression. (pp. viii–ix)

Therefore, technocratic science, through its methods, is distanced from first-hand experience and meaning. Merleau-Ponty asserted that science does not have the same significance as our everyday experience of the world because

> it is a rationale or explanation of that world. . . . Scientific points of view, according to which my existence is a moment of the world's, are always the same time both naive and dishonest, because they take for granted . . . the other point of view, namely that of consciousness, through which from the outset a world forms itself round me and begins to exist for me. (pp. viii–ix)

Most practitioners of Western science simply take social reality for granted without any deeper investigation. Instead, they try to suppress social influences in formal investigations, calling them "biases" that will undermine validity. Yet in a field like education, where all phenomena involve social action, it is impossible to remove the social dimension. Schutz (1954) cautioned social scientists that if their task was to describe the "life-worlds" of social actors, then they need to be wary of replacing the viewpoint of everyday actors with a fictional, abstracted world constructed by scientific observers using positivist methods. Instead, he suggested that primary research attention be directed toward exploring individuals' viewpoints.

Although arguments about the social versus technocratic nature of knowledge were central in the early development of the social sciences, students of educational research are rarely, if ever, introduced to this debate. According to Schutz (1954), this has been "a controversy which for more than half a century has split not only logicians and methodologists but also social scientists into two schools of thought" (p. 257). On one hand, technocratic researchers have argued that "the methods of the natural sciences which have brought about such magnificent results are the only scientific ones, and that they alone, therefore, have to be applied in their entirety to the study of human affairs" (Schutz, 1954, p. 257). Failure to do so, say technocratic researchers, has prevented the social sciences from developing overarching systems of explanatory theory comparable in power and precision to those offered by the natural sciences.

On the other hand, rejecting the idea that social sciences should adopt the methods of the natural sciences, Husserl (1960) argued that the unreflective application of the scientific method in constructing the "sciences of human life" has not only failed but distorted the phenomena being studied. He suggested that this failure cannot be overcome by more sophisticated development of the methods and techniques of the natural sciences:

> It has already become clear to us that an "exact" psychology, as an analogue to physics . . . is an absurdity. . . . In no way can a science of souls be modeled on natural science or seek methodological counsel from it. It can only model itself on its own subject matter. (Husserl, 1960, p. 223)

Bernstein (1976) added that if it is claimed that

> a "genuine" psychology is not a "science of souls," but a science of observable behavior, this does not weaken Husserl's charge, for psychology [or any social science] conceived in this manner will never be able to illuminate the structures of human subjectivity and intersubjectivity. (p. 133)

Husserl (1960), Bernstein (1976), Merleau-Ponty (1962), and Schutz (1954, 1967) agree that a different, socially focused foundation is necessary for the entire range of the sciences of human life, as well as a new understanding of the character of those sciences. Applying an intersubjective understanding, though, adds considerable complexity to the task of social science research. An appropriate social scientific method, Schutz (1954) maintained, must shift from rote applications of physical science to an approach that involves in all aspects of methodology those constructs and experiences drawn from everyday human social reality.

The positivist view that arm's-length observation of overt human behavior is the only valid scientific investigation of social reality severely limits researchers to a small sector of the social world—situations that can be directly observed and measured. Yet there are many other dimensions of the social world—including customs, common interpretations, institutions, shared routines, habitualizations, roles in social processes, and the division of labor—that constitute the vast majority of schooling experience. Educational researchers need research practices that allow them to investigate the changing social and intersubjective contexts of teaching, learning, communication, language, evaluation, and policy—none of which can be studied sufficiently through technocratic methods. The one-sided presentation of research methods and the lack of any substantive introduction to philosophies of science, phenomenology, and other critical scholarship maintain the scientistic hierarchy in social science research and leave educators in a binary trap that limits their inquiry practices.

References

Apel, K. O. (1984). *Understanding and explanation: A transcendental and pragmatic perspective.* MIT Press.

Apple, M. (1998). Are markets and standards democratic? *Educational Researcher, 27*(6), 24–28.

Ayer, A. J. (1936). *Language, truth, and logic.* Gollancz.

Barad, K. (2007). *Meeting the universe halfway: Quantum physics and the entanglement of matter and meaning.* Duke University Press.

Baudrillard, J. (1988). *Jean Baudrillard: Selected writings.* Stanford University Press.

Berger, P., & Luckmann, T. (1966). *The social construction of reality: A treatise in the sociology of knowledge.* Penguin Books.

Bernstein, R. J. (1976). *The restructuring of social and political theory.* University of Pennsylvania Press.

Bridgman, P. (1927). *The logic of modern physics.* Macmillan Publishers.

Chomsky, N. (1975). *The logical structure of linguistic theory.* Plenum Press.

Common Core State Standards Initiative. (n.d.). *Mission statement.* http://www.corestandards.org

Endacott, J. L., Wright, G. P., Goering, C. Z., Collet, V. S., Denny, G. S., & Davis, J. J. (2015). Robots teaching other little robots: Neoliberalism, CCSS, and teacher professionalism. *Review of Education, Pedagogy, and Cultural Studies, 37*(5), 414–437.

Erickson, F., & Gutierrez, K. (2002). Comment: Culture, rigor, and science in educational research. *Educational Researcher, 31*(8), 21–24.

Feyerabend, P. (1975). *Against method.* Verso.

Gadamer, H. G. (1976). *Philosophical hermeneutics.* University of California Press.

Green, C. D. (2001). Operationism again: What did Bridgman say? What did Bridgman need? *Theory & Psychology, 11*(1), 45–51.

Habermas, J. (1971). *Knowledge and human interests.* Beacon Press.

Haraway, D. (2004). *The Haraway reader.* Routledge.

Harding, S. (1998). *Is science multicultural: Postcolonialisms, feminisims, and epistemologies.* Indiana University Press.

Harris, M. (1979). *Cultural materialism: The struggle for a science of culture.* Random House.

Hemphill, D., & Blakely, E. (2015). *Language, nation, and identity in the classroom: Legacies of modernity and colonialism in schooling.* Peter Lang.

Husserl, E. (1960). *Cartesian meditations: An introduction to phenomenology.* Martinus Nijhoff.

Hussey, T., & Smith, P. (2002). The trouble with learning outcomes. *Active Learning in Higher Education, 3*(3), 220–233.

Klees, S. J. (2008). A quarter century of neoliberal thinking in education: Misleading analyses and failed policies. *Globalisation, Societies and Education, 6*(4), 311–348.

Kuhn, T. S. (1969). *The structure of scientific revolutions.* University of Chicago Press.

Kvale, S. (1976). The psychology of learning as ideology and technology. *Behaviorism, 4*(1), 97–116.

Lave, J., & McDermott, R. (2002). Estranged labor learning. *Outlines. Critical Practice Studies, 4*(1), 19–48.

Levine, T. R., Weber, R., Hullett, C., Park, H. S., & Massi Lindsay, L. L. (2008). A critical assessment of null hypothesis significance testing in quantitative communication research. *Human Communication Research, 34*(2), 171–187.

Lyotard, J. (1999). *The postmodern condition: A report on knowledge.* The University of Minnesota Press.

Marx, K. (1971). *Capital: Vol. I. A critical analysis of capitalist production.* Progress Publishers. (Original work published 1887)

McDermott, R. P. (1996). The acquisition of a child by a learning disability. In S. Chaiklin & J. Lave (Eds.), *Understanding practice: Perspectives on activity and context* (pp. 269–305). Cambridge University Press.

Mehta, J. D. (2013). The penetration of technocratic logic into the educational field: Rationalizing schooling from the progressives to the present. *Teachers College Record, 113*(5), 1–40.

Merleau-Ponty, M. (1962). *Phenomenology of perception.* Humanities Press.

National Institute of Child Health and Human Development. (2000). *Report of the National Reading Panel. Teaching children to read: An evidence-based assessment of the scientific research literature on reading and its implications for reading instruction* (NIH Publication No. 00-4769). U.S. Government Printing Office.

Needham, J. (1954). *Science and civilization in China: Volume I.* Cambridge University Press.

Nelson, D., Joseph, G. G., & Williams, G. (1993). *Multicultural mathematics: Teaching mathematics from a global perspective*. Oxford University Press.

Pearson, P. D. (2004). The reading wars. *Educational Policy, 18*(1), 216–252.

Popper, K. (1963). *Conjectures and refutations: The growth of scientific knowledge*. Routledge.

Popper, K. (1968). *The logic of scientific discovery*. Harper & Row.

Purcell-Gates, V., Duke, N. K, & Martineau, J. A. (2007). Learning to read and write genre-specific text: Roles of authentic experience and explicit teaching. *Reading Research Quarterly, 42*(1), 8–45.

Russell, L. J. (1928). Review of Bridgman's *The Logic of Modern Physics*. *Mind, 37*, 355–361.

Schutz, A. (1954). Concept and theory formation in the social sciences. *The Journal of Philosophy, 51*(9), 257–273.

Schutz, A. (1967). *The phenomenology of the social world*. Northwestern University Press.

Skinner, B. F. (1957). *Verbal behavior*. Appleton-Century-Crofts.

Sparks, S. D. (2012). New research thinking girds core. *Education Week, 32*(12), 6–9.

Tienkin, C. H. (2013). Neoliberalism, social Darwinism, and consumerism masquerading as school reform. *Interchange, 43*(4), 295–316.

U.S. Department of Education. (2019). *Institute of Education Sciences: Mission and vision. Grants.* https://www.grants.gov/learn-grants/grant-making-agencies/department-of-education.html

Watson, J. (1913). Psychology as the behaviorist views it. *Psychological Review, 20*(2), 158–177.

TWO

Challenging Binary Logic

THE SCIENTIFIC APPROACH ADAPTED BY the social sciences separates verifiable observable behavior in a binary way from unverifiable inner states (purposes, emotions). Influenced by Descartes's (1967) early attempt to chart existence systematically in two dimensions (x/y axis, mind/body binary), Western modernist thinkers of the Enlightenment articulated a division between the mind (nonmaterial or metaphysical) and the body (material). This internal/external dichotomy grounded the development of the scientific method, as it made possible the assumption that there is an external world outside the mind that can be empirically known, objectively measured, and materially manipulated. The division of science from social and other ways of knowing, along with many other seemingly natural divisions (self/Other, body/mind), is neither inevitable nor neutral. Binaries exaggerate differences, ignoring continua that may exist between two poles. Binaries can also be hierarchical, with one side considered "less than" the other. In educational research, binary thinking—particularly the rigid divisions between objective and subjective forms of knowledge, or quantitative versus qualitative data—limits what is possible and contributes to the inequitable status quo.

2.1 Postmodern perspectives.

When postmodernism is discussed at all in research methods texts, it is treated as the binary opposite of objective, empirical work. In one text, for example, the authors spend two paragraphs treating postmodernism simplistically in their sole chapter on qualitative research. At the beginning of the chapter, there is a cartoon clip art image of researchers discussing two supposedly contradictory approaches: "You quantitative researchers are so preoccupied with control that you never see the big picture!" versus "You qualitative researchers are so subjective, you never can be sure what you've found or where it applies!" (Fraenkel et al., 2012, p. 424). Through this reductive dichotomization, the authors make the assumption that a postmodern approach to research will result in studies that are entirely subjective and therefore of limited value. Few, if any, references in research methods texts substantively explore postmodernism or apply it to educational research design. Yet Grewal and Kaplan (1994) have argued that postmodernity is "an immensely powerful and useful conception that gives us an opportunity to analyze the way that a culture of modernity is produced in diverse locations and how these cultural productions are circulated, distributed, received, and . . . commodified" (p. 5).

Like many binaries, the objective/subjective divide—foundational to technocratic research—is frequently blurred in practice. The distinction between objective and subjective knowledge is discursive, owing primarily to conceptual and linguistic forms of representation rather than to any intrinsic content. Barthes (1981) questioned the distinction between objective and subjective, asking if scientific texts "really differ, in some specific trait, in some indubitably distinctive feature, from imaginary narration as we find in the epic, the novel, the drama?" (p. 1). Lyotard (1999) also challenged the objective/subjective binary, arguing that scientific discourse—like fiction—relies on narrative argumentation for legitimation. Scientific narratives adhere to a particular expected form laid out in journal articles or reports, where authors provide an abstract, specify hypotheses, cite previous literature, document methods, present analysis and summaries, and situate findings in relation to prior knowledge claims. Empirical data and scientific findings are constantly narrativized. Scientific reporting is simply one of many types of discourse, no more or less valid than any other discourse.

Challenging the claims of objectivity in science, scholars in the latter decades of the 20th century developed a body of thought known as **postmodernism**. Postmodernism denotes a radical shift away from the system of values and practices of modernity, in particular a departure from the metanarrative of science as the foundation of all knowledge. The postmodern perspective emerged from multiple disciplines and became influential in the humanities, though it remains marginalized in the social sciences. The term *postmodern* was first applied to architecture, then to art, where it was used to represent a new epoch or style, and subsequently to literature, history, and other humanities. Contrary to its reductive characterization in research texts, postmodernism represents neither a negation of all modernist forms of research logic and scientific knowledge production nor an overcoming of them. Postmodernists generally call into question the values of Western rationality, logic, and science, but they do not argue automatically against the worth of these values; postmodernity is not a complete negation of the past.

By no means a unitary school of thought, postmodernity primarily challenges Western metanarratives. Many postmodernists "call the heritage of European thought into question without proposing the means for a critical 'overcoming'" (Peters & Besley, 2006, p. 41). Postmodernism defies the metanarrative of progress, which suggests that knowledge constantly accumulates, advancing thought, democracy, and civilization. It rejects the linear logic that its very name (as a "post" condition) suggests. The use of the prefix "post-" in *postmodernity* indicates taking leave of modernity's metanarratives. As Lyotard (1999) suggested, postmodernism does not signify "the end of modernism, but another relation to modernism" (p. 79).

Lyotard (1999) defined as modern "any science that legitimates itself with reference to a metadiscourse of this kind making an explicit appeal to some grand narrative," following the logic that "that the whole is determinable" (pp. xxiii, xxiv). This logic leads to the hubristic Western belief that everything can be understood from the single rational methodological system of science. Lyotard suggested that metanarratives are a hallmark of Western modernity, defining them as "the stories that cultures tell themselves about their own practices and beliefs in order to legitimate them. They function as a unified story that purports to legitimate or found a set of practices, a cultural self-image, discourse, or institution" (as cited in Peters, 1999, p. 123).

It was not until the late 20th and early 21st centuries that modernist metanarratives were seriously called into question on a broad scale. New forms of circulation of capital through multinational corporations and the emergence of a consumer society shifted power away from the nation-state. Globalized information technology, media, and service industries replaced manufacturing as the major economic force. Further transformations included

- the emergence of transnational corporations,
- the development of global information and telecommunications technologies,
- the substitution of transnational capital for labor in the global industrial economy,
- the decentering of the West,
- the expansion of diasporic flows,

- the commodification of everyday life,
- the collapse of distinctions between high and popular culture, and
- the growth of youth cultures.

"The nature of knowledge cannot," Lyotard (1999) argued, "survive unchanged within this context of general transformation" (p. 4).

The postmodern position is not a call for the irrational or the dismantling of all scientific inquiry; instead, it is a critique of the central position science holds as the only or most valid form of absolute knowledge. "There is, in short, nothing wrong with the hopes of the Enlightenment," wrote Rorty (1991), "the hopes which created the Western democracies. . . . There is only something wrong with the attempt to [demonstrate] the 'objective' superiority of our way of life over all other alternatives" (p. 34).

Some accounts of postmodernism attribute its genesis to Nietzsche, who suggested metaphorically that "God is dead." "That is to say," Heidegger explained,

> [the] "Christian God" [that] . . . stands for the "transcendent" in general in its various meanings—for "ideals" and "norms," "principles," and "rules," "ends" and "values," which are set "above" the being, in order to give being a whole, a purpose, and order. (as cited in Peters & Besley, 2006, p. 40)

Nietzsche's statement became a starting point for a reassessment of overarching value systems. "Incredulity toward metanarratives" is one of the most often-cited characterizations of postmodernism (Lyotard, 1999, p. xxiv).

Any account that claims to be objective, factual, or scientific actually relies, many postmodernist theorists argue, on metaphors and other fictional, imaginative devices; thus, truth is not an objective process of deduction. The production of truth, Foucault (1984) argued, is a social, discursive construction. Instead of trying to discover what is scientifically true and what is not, Foucault (1984) investigated "historically how effects of truth are produced within discourses which in themselves are neither true or false" (p. 60).

Truth, from Foucault's (1980) perspective, is not something discovered through scientific methods. He referred to the mechanisms used to produce regimes of truth as **power/knowledge**. The individual, for instance, is conceived by Foucault as a "truth-effect of systems of power/knowledge that are culturally and historically specific rather than being something that exists in an essential sense" (Sullivan, 2003, p. 81). Power/knowledge operates in the field of education through the ensemble of rules distributed in manuals of diagnostic criteria for psychological disorders, assessments, and behavioral checklists. These diagnostic tools produce the neurological, biological, and medical evidence for establishing categories of learners (attention-deficit disordered, dyslexic, or gifted and talented). These regimes of truth work to naturalize and universalize rigid categories, hiding their historical origins as invented constructions.

To illustrate how power/knowledge operates, Foucault investigated the ways that various institutions—asylums, hospitals, and prisons—discipline subjects through the production of regimes of truth. Through analyzing the production and distribution of hegemonic discourses, Foucault related how institutions have effectively shaped and controlled entire populations. He used the term **biopower** to refer to the specific administrative forms of power that optimize human capabilities for the benefit of the state. Biopower has historically operated through a diverse range of techniques and regulatory discourses such as birthrate, longevity, public health, housing, and migration.

This form of administrative power, what Foucault referred to as **governmentality**, focuses on generating the capacities of individuals—following the logic of capitalism—rather than impeding them, making them submit, or destroying them. Governmentality emerged in the West as "the way in which political power now manages and regulates populations and goods . . . the main way state power is vitalized" (Butler, 2004, p. 51). Governmentality operates through policies and bureaucracies of the state and nonstate institutions, and through discourses that are legitimated, Butler (2004) observed, "neither by direct elections nor through established authority" (p. 52). The tactics of governmentality operate diffusely to order populations, their practices, and their beliefs in relation to specific policy goals. These state policies, along with the discourses of the social and medical sciences, define individuals and work to control their conduct.

In education, governmentality operates via assessment systems, attendance policies, behavioral management systems, high-stakes assessments, and numerous other means of regulating student behavior. Schools, Foucault (1977) argued, like other "disciplinary institutions" provide "a machinery of control that functions like a microscope of conduct; the fine, analytical divisions that they create formed around [individuals] an apparatus of observation, recording and training" (p. 173). This apparatus functions to create and maintain specific kinds of subjectivities, or individual's perceptions of their own reality and selfhood.

In contrast to modernists such as Marx, who investigate power in a linear, hierarchical fashion by looking at which social groupings (classes) hold dominant positions, Foucault analyzed how power operates through networks of discourses that produce individuals: "Power must be analyzed as something that circulates . . . power is employed and exercised through a net-like organization . . . not only do individuals circulate between its threads, they are always in the position of simultaneously undergoing and exercising this power" (Foucault, 1980, pp. 98–99). This netlike organization of power is apparent in schools, where teachers are both empowered to exercise control over their students and classrooms and disempowered via administrative constraints, scheduling requirements, the division of academic disciplines, instructional minute matrices, scripted curricula, standards-based assessments, and other forms of power/knowledge.

Applying Foucault's analysis makes visible the ways that multiple institutions in the West establish how children are viewed, seen to develop, and acted on as subjects (Foucault, 1988). These institutions—schools, pediatrics, parent education forums, juvenile delinquency programs, the toy industry, and media corporations—produce a normative discourse of childhood. Processes of **normalization** establish certain arrangements, identities, and relationships as common-sense or natural. These normative configurations are enforced through standardized curriculum, assessment packages, classroom management practices, and other school policies that promote conforming behaviors and exclude "abnormal" students by placing them in remedial or intervention programs. The normal/abnormal binary is widely seen as an inevitable, universal construct, yet Foucault's historical studies of the conceptualization of madness (2006), illness (1973), criminality (1977), and sexuality (1990) show vast differences over time in the discourses used to describe these norms. Through processes of normalization, schools and other disciplinary institutions produce many categories of identity as natural or biological.

Even the most seemingly neutral tasks such as helping students attain proficiency in basic skills involve the constitution, normalization, and subjugation of individuals. The attention in schools to student performance is paired with the constant assessment of individual traits, as teachers help produce learners who participate with classroom materials in "meaningful, productive" ways, engaging in "appropriate" behaviors. Literacy instruction, for example, involves not just teaching reading and writing, Hammerberg (2004) argued, but developing "certain modes of training and modification of individuals, not only in the obvious sense of acquiring certain skills but also in the sense of acquiring certain attitudes" (p. 18).

Hammerberg investigated how young children become "independent learners" through normalization and the material conditions of the learning space. Preschool and kindergarten teachers, Hammerberg reported, typically spend the first six weeks of school training students in how to use reading centers. They introduce the centers one at a time and role-play how to behave appropriately in each. While teachers work one-on-one with students or in small groups, they expect the rest of the class to be meaningfully engaged in the specifically prepared environment, selecting books from leveled bins, reading with a buddy in a book nook, or gluing letters to paper. To an outside observer the students appear to be self-directed and acting independently, though every aspect of conduct is described and trained in minute detail.

The problem is not, Hammerberg (2004) suggested, that self-regulated independence is "necessarily bad" but that the "techniques used to govern oneself in the learning environment are internalized in such a way that they are described as a part of a private self, as opposed to part of the system" (p. 374). Desired attributes of students are naturalized instead of understood as socially prepared and organized, making "an individual into an object of case study in terms of psychological norms" (Hammerberg, 2004, p. 376).

In schools, students are defined in relation to normalized binaries: responsible/irresponsible, motivated/unmotivated, attentive/distracted. Through training and other normalizing discourses, teachers also maintain not only abstract binaries but also accepted "natural" divides, such as drawing static lines between genders. The discourses that accompany gender divisions in schools and the media are robust and filled with normative pressure to maintain a strict binary, each with its own attendant roles, themes, and props. Separation along gender lines is constantly enforced in the daily practices of schools, where students are divided boy/girl to stand in line or form teams.

Arguing that gender is not a fact of nature, Butler (1993) used Foucault's notion of discourse as being productive to show how gender is produced and performed. She advanced an account of gender—and identity more generally—as performative:

> Gender is not a performance that a prior subject elects to do, but gender is performative in the sense that it constitutes as an effect the very subject it appears to express. It is a compulsory performance. . . . It may be that the very categories of sex, of sexual identity, of gender are produced or maintained in the effects of this compulsory performance, effects which are disingenuously named as causes, origins, disingenuously lined up within a causal or expressive sequence that the heterosexual norm produces to legitimate itself as the origin of all sex. (Butler, 1993, pp. 315, 318)

In Butler's concept of **performativity**, she proposed that gender is not an essence or a composite of attributes but rather a "doing": "Gender is itself a kind of becoming or activity . . . gender ought not to be conceived of as a noun or a substantial thing or static cultural marker, but rather as an incessant and repeated action" (as cited in Barad, 2003, p. 808).

Gender is the performative effect of acts repeated through a rigid regulatory frame and "congeal over time to produce the appearance of a substance, of a natural sort of being" (Butler 1999, p. 33). Or as Haraway (1991) argued, "There is nothing about being female that naturally binds women together into a unified category. There is not even such a state as 'being' female, itself a highly complex category constructed in contested sexual scientific discourses and other social practices" (p. 155).

Butler (1993) sought to understand how identities are produced. According to Hall (1996), she wanted to see how

> the subject is produced in the course of its materialization . . . strongly grounded in a performative theory of language and the subject . . . re-read not as the act by which a subject brings into being what she/he names but rather as that reiterative power of discourse to produce the phenomena that it regulates and constrains. (p. 14)

Performing the self entails the obligation to do gender or other identities not as an act of intentionality but as performance already set up by a pre-scripted rehearsal. Homosexuality, drag, or other subversions of norms, for instance, work to expose "the causal lines as retrospectively and performatively produced fabrications" (Butler, 1993, p. 31). Butler (1999), following Foucault, asserted that systems of power produce the subjects they come to represent. "The subjects regulated by such structures, are, by virtue of being subjected to them, formed, defined, and reproduced in accordance with the requirements of those structures" (p. 2).

2.2 Histories of dialectical thinking.

Despite their feeling of inevitability, most binaries unravel upon investigation. In all high/low cultural determinations, for instance high culture versus popular culture,

> a recurrent pattern emerges: the "top" attempts to reject and eliminate the "bottom" for reasons of prestige and status, only to discover that it is in some way frequently dependent on that low-Other . . . but also that the top *includes* that low symbolically. (Stallybrass & White, 1986, p. 5)

Each side is dependent on the other, yet the low-Other is "denied at the level of . . . social being whilst it is instrumentally constitutive of the shared imaginary repertoires of the dominant culture" (Stallybrass & White, 1986, p. 6). Although binary divides are deeply normalized throughout Western cultures and educational systems, there is a long global history of dialectical systems of thought that do not start with rigid dualities.

Dialectical thinking merges binary, opposing thoughts to blend two opposing poles of meaning to synthesize new, hybrid meanings. This approach is found in Asian and Indigenous cultures in a variety of constructs, and in the West in dialectical, pragmatic, and agential realist theories. Dialectical thinking appears, for instance, in Chinese cognitive and philosophical traditions in Daoist teachings, which are pervasive in Chinese thought and everyday life: "Lu Xun, a prominent modern Chinese author of the early 20th century, claimed that all roots of Chinese thinking are in the Daoist tradition" (Peng et al., 2006, p. 249).

Daoism is generally reduced in the West to a few catchphrases about the mystic wisdom of the *Dao De Jing* ("Book of Changes"), yet the philosophy of Daoism is comprehensive and concerned with understanding the nature of the world and knowledge. Daoism emphasizes living in harmony with the unplanned rhythms of the universe—called the *Dao*, which means "the way" or "the path." Daoist ethics emphasize *wu wei* (action without intention), naturalness, simplicity, spontaneity, and the "three treasures" of compassion, frugality, and humility. Laozi, the scholar who conceived of the *Dao*, suggested that it operates through the dialectical interaction of *Yin* and *Yang*. *Yin* represents the negative, passive, and feminine, whereas *Yang* signifies the positive, active, and masculine. Unlike Western binary logic, these two sides are not seen as separate. Neither *Yin* or *Yang* can exist without the other, and neither is inferior to the other. Existence entails a dialectical interaction between the two.

Another dialectical belief of Daoism—nonduality—states that matter is spirit and spirit is matter. "The Dao is at once the void and all matter that confronts us" (Peng et al., 2006, p. 250). All things in the universe are seen, too, as perpetually changing in orderly cycles. Peng et al. (2006) suggest that

> The Chinese model of explanation presupposes a part-whole approach. Thus, parts exist only within wholes, with which they have inseparable relations. As applied to people, the Chinese perspective rejects an atomistic explanation of individuals' behaviors, and instead refers to individuals' relations to some whole, such as the family, society, Dao, principles, or pure consciousness. (p. 257)

Multiple researchers (Munro, 1985; Needham, 1954; Peng et al., 2006) emphasize the dialectical nature of Chinese philosophy and everyday life.

Dialectical reasoning may also be found in numerous Indigenous cultures. Some speakers of Andean languages, for instance, describe opposites as complementary and interdependent—instead of antagonistic (good versus evil, mind over matter) (Webb, 2012). They use the word *yanantin* to describe the concept of "complementary opposites" or "pairing" and refer to the "active process by which the *yanantin* pair becomes paired" as *masintin* (Webb, 2012, p. 75). The process of pairing is a multistaged movement toward complementarity that includes the stages of meeting, boundary testing, union, and separation. However, *masintin* is neither a utopian endpoint nor a harmonious wholeness in perfect balance or peace. Resolving tensions does not necessarily lead, as in much of Western thought, to a superior element. "The complementary perspective calls for an acknowledgment that each side of the equation plays an essential role in the unfolding and enfolding of the whole" (Webb,

2012, p. 86). The dialectical nature of Andean thought creates a context, a "field of the middle," in which "third things" can emerge.

There is also a dialectical tradition in the West that first emerged in classical Greece to describe philosophical argumentation involving contradictions between opposing sides. Plato portrayed dialectics as a back-and-forth dialogue. Many centuries later, Hegel employed dialectical reasoning to articulate the conceptual unification of apparent opposites, where "two apparently opposed ideas—because of their strife and not despite it—become first reconciled and then unified" (Webb, 2012, p. 81). This is the process by which an initial premise—a thesis—encounters a contradictory opposite—an antithesis—and ultimately moves toward synthesis.

Consciousness, according to Hegel, does not become self-conscious until it encounters another to interact with and distinguish itself. A struggle ensues between thesis and antithesis until a synthesis emerges—"a 'third thing' that both contains and transcends the thesis and antithesis, constituting a higher form of consciousness than either of the original two created separately" (Webb, 2012, p. 82). Synthesis is not something, Hegel argued, that suddenly appears but something that "shows itself only in the end . . . in such a way that this end reveals that [it] has also been there from the beginning" (as cited in Webb, 2012, p. 82). The new "crystallized truth" of synthesis becomes a new thesis that will encounter an antithesis, and the cycle will continue:

> Dialectic is thus the very process of thinking, where thought "loses itself in" and becomes "entangled in the contradiction" of its nonidentity with its object, and yet where this very negativity urges thought to "persevere," to "work out itself the solution to its own contradiction." It is . . . a series of successive "conversions" whereby the relation of consciousness to the world is progressively transformed. (Berthold-Bond, 1989, pp. 84–85)

Hegel showed how something realizes itself in relation to something else; it is often dependent on its opposite. The self, for example, is conceived of only when it is related to the "other." Hegel maintained that it is primarily through participating in a community that people begin to think of themselves as individuals, and as certain kinds of individuals. Through noticing the other, they begin to understand themselves. "For Hegel the individual self is in no sense an immediately given element of consciousness; rather, the individual becomes a subject through being in relationships with others" (Nielsen, 2016, p. 148). He described a state of "becoming"—a state that exists between "being" and "nothingness."

Marx (1887/1971) applied Hegel's dialectic to material conditions (class, labor, and socioeconomic relations) to develop the theory of dialectical materialism, which shows how the individual and society are interactively connected rather than isolated and separable. Marx proposed a dialectical synthesis where individuals are "always material and embodied in the local practices in which they participate, and in their relations with other persons, things, and institutional arrangements" (Rasmussen, 2016, p. 231). This means that social context is not simply a backdrop to individual behaviors but a constitutive element. For educators this involves seeing the ways that social and individual dimensions of practice are inseparable; it "means that we need to understand learning as within the frames of developing a specific identity and at the same time maintaining and changing communities of practices" (Nielsen, 2016, p. 155).

Marx (1887/1971) did not deny that things exist but argued that the core notion of them is a cluster of relations rather than a set of independent, unchanging factors. A commodity, for instance, is not simply a thing but a complex relation of consumption and production. In Marx's dialectical view, things gain their meaning from the relationship or tension between presumed opposites: "Production is at the same time consumption, and consumption is at the same time production" (as cited in Ollman, 1976, p. 16). The two are dependent on each other and define themselves in relation to each other. Many phenomena such as self and other, Marx argued, are dependent on their binary opposite as a way of defining themselves.

For Marx, "the basic unit of reality is not a thing but a Relation" (Ollman, 1976, p. 69). Although society creates the conditions for the individual, the individual is not entirely determined by these conditions. The individual is both subject to the conditions of the society and an agential co-creator of those same conditions. Thus, Marx dissolved the individual/society binary by making the relation between them "the irreducible minimum of all units" (Ollman, 1976, p. 14). As Engels extended the argument, "the atom itself is nothing more than a Relation" (as cited in Ollman, 1976, p. 27).

By taking relation as the primary unit of reality, Marx "bridge[d] the fact-value, cause-effect, and nature-society distinctions which characterize the common sense view of reality" (Ollman, 1976, p. 69). He dissolved binaries by arguing that any function is both objective (present in the world) and subjective (there because it has been identified and named). Facts and values, Marx argued, cannot be separated: "To accept that reality is halved in this way is to admit failure from the start. . . . The logical distinction between facts and values is founded on the belief that it is possible to conceive of one without the other" (Ollman, 1976, p. 45). Yet, values are based on the way facts are perceived and could not exist apart from them. This means more than simply that facts affect our values, or that values affect what are considered to be the facts. Facts always include values and values include facts: "Each includes the other and is part of what is meant by the other's concept . . . to split their union into logically distinct halves is to distort their real character" (Ollman, 1976, p. 46).

As Ollman (1976) articulated further, "Other people viewing the same 'raw facts' with another conceptual scheme may not even observe" the same relation (p. 25). There are no stable, unchanging entities or absolute values that researchers can discover or apply. Causes and effects, too, are unstable, as relations are always in flux and dependent on various interactions and contexts. "Hence," Dietzgen wrote, "any thing that is torn out of its contextual relations ceases to exist" (as cited in Ollman, 1976, p. 37).

It is a common assumption among researchers that one can "group social phenomena into easily separable units in order that one (or one set of them) can be held to be primary" (Ollman, 1976, p. 10). This leads to the "endless attempts to account for causality and the accompanying need to distinguish between cause and condition" (Ollman, 1976, p. 16). Marx instead conceived of causes and conditions as internally and dialectically related. Each social factor is related to its own historical forms, as well as to the constantly changing, surrounding factors.

Taking a dialectical approach to inquiry, then, means searching for the "internal relations within and between abstracted units" (Ollman, 1976, p. 65). For example, researchers might think dialectically about how "high" and "low" readers exist only because of the other, how they emerge in and through each other, what material conditions create this abstraction, and what interests are served in this separation. Using relation as the smallest unit of analysis, Ollman (1976) suggested, can help account for "the changes and uncertainties that constitute so large a part of social life" (p. 16). To see things relationally means recognizing that phenomena and contexts are not fixed but changing. They do not have an essence and a stable location in one clear-cut category; they can be viewed in continual motion. Instead of asking how an instructional technique or other isolated variable affects a social group, the question for educational researchers becomes how relations are produced in and through one another, including both material conditions and social/discursive constructions.

2.3 Pragmatism.

The philosophical perspective of **pragmatism** offers a further dialectical challenge to the internal/external binary division that underlies positivists' belief that science can measure an external reality or "things as they really are." Pragmatism originated primarily in the work of three American philosophers: Dewey (1922), Pierce (1955), and James (1907). Kant originally used the term *practical* to describe a situation where knowledge and action are separate and used *pragmatic* to describe a situation where knowledge and action are connected. For pragmatic philosophers there is a dialogical connection between knowledge and action (Biesta & Burbules, 2003). Reality, pragmatists argue, reveals itself only as a result of activity or transactions between person and environment. Dewey maintained, for instance, that it is a mistake to categorize an arm as part of an organism's body but the food they ingest as separate: "Both the arm and the food are actually part of the organism's life functions in the same way that gravity and countless other things usually regarded as external belong to the organism" (Brinkmann, 2013, p. 48). Dewey thus rejected the Cartesian mind/body or internal/external divide and saw both person and environment as elements of a larger system of time and space. Dewey defined reality instead as "the world as we experience it" (Morgenbesser, 1977).

Dewey's work can help researchers move toward understanding knowledge as an intersubjective construction, similar to the claims of social phenomenologists:

> By showing that objectivity is simply not possible, that subjectivity is not always a problem, and that intersubjectivity addresses those instances where the subjectivity of knowledge does become a problem, Dewey presents us

> with a position that helps to overcome the stalemate between objectivism and subjectivism. (Biesta, 2014, p. 43)

Dewey's work recognized that knowledge is plural, shifting, conflictual, and partial, without abandoning the idea of inquiry and observation as tools for learning more about the world. Knowledge for Dewey is constructed pragmatically through experience. For instance, the meaning of a concept, like "hard" or "soft," comes from the experience of handling a substance and seeing if it is scratched by other substances. Only from testing or acting on substances or phenomena can their differences emerge.

Dewey showed how social and educational conditions have been oversimplified by use of psychological dualisms, such as stimulus/response, arguing that there is only an artificial separation between the two. The concepts of stimulus and response do not need to be abandoned entirely, Dewey argued, but they need to be reconceptualized as "divisions of labor"—a "reflex arc." He suggested that sensory stimuli and motor responses should not be viewed "as separate and complete entities in themselves, but as divisions of labor, functioning factors, within the single concrete whole" (Dewey, 1896, p. 358). A stimulus (like a loud sound) and a motor response (running away) are not separate physical entities, Dewey (1896) asserted, but "are always inside a coordination and have their significance purely from the part played in maintaining or reconstituting the coordination" (p. 360). In technocratic logic, a loud sound is considered the stimulus, which proceeds and is separate from a startled response. Yet if someone is startled by a noise, then that noise *is* startling. This has nothing to do with the external qualities of the sound, its volume, proximity, or tone. The sound is startling because it startled someone.

Any analysis that is limited to the stimulus/response dualism, then, is incomplete, disjointed, and fragmented. The problem with this division, Dewey (1896) said, is that it always ignores the conditions or context—for example, what happened prior to the stimulus:

> If one is reading a book, if one is hunting, if one is watching in a dark place on a lonely night, if one is performing a chemical experiment, in each case, the noise . . . is a different experience. . . . The "stimulus" emerges out of this. . . . Prior activity influences the value of the sensation. . . . The sound is not a mere stimulus, or mere sensation; it again is an act, that of hearing. . . . Just as the

> "response" is necessary to constitute the stimulus, to determine it as sound and as this kind of sound . . . so the sound experience must persist as a value in the running, to keep it up, to control it. (pp. 361–363)

What is real, according to Dewey, is not what is "out there" in the external world but what is experienced. What matters is not capturing as accurately as possible what is happening but discovering the conditions and consequences of its happening. Unlike the one-way, closed stimulus-response model of behaviorism, where a change of external factor results in a fixed internal change, Dewey offered a **transactional** model of continuous readjustment. In this transactional model, the stimulus is not something that comes from the outside and causes a student to change or sets a student in motion. The stimulus is instead understood as a change in the environment connected to a change in activity. A stimulus can be identified only retrospectively as an ordered sequence of acts that, working together, led to a specific end. A stimulus becomes a stimulus only when something responds to it; they are mutually constituted. Dewey deconstructed the entrenched stimulus-response binary and exposed the basic problem of establishing causality in technocratic research.

Dewey (1896) was not discouraged that causality cannot be conclusively demonstrated, nor did he accept that the contingency of all things must lead to rejecting reason and progress. Instead, he asserted that language, self, and communities are contingent and always changing, and that it is possible through inquiry to find practical, concrete, and reasonable responses to problems. While it may not be possible through research to discover a universal truth, it is possible to discover a temporal truth. In this, Dewey turned away from the immutable "laws" of Western science that are claimed to apply in all times and places. Instead, he turned toward such pre-Enlightenment, Renaissance humanists as Montaigne and Erasmus, who tolerated uncertainty, ambiguity, and diversity of opinion while promoting practical temporal truths. As Toulmin (1990) argued, "We should try to recapture the practical modesty of the humanists, which let them live free of anxiety, despite uncertainty, ambiguity, and pluralism" (p. 105).

Since causality can point in multiple directions, the only way for teachers to find out how to proceed is to try out different lines of action. Educational researchers often specify the stimulus (the kind of curriculum or technique) before they begin their studies, yet the stimulus only appears when students respond. When a teacher hits on an adequate response, then coordination is achieved, and they can identify the stimulus.

Pragmatism and other forms of dialectical thinking offer a means of critiquing the ahistorical rationality of Western science without "descending into intellectual paralysis ('What can we do now that we've seen the changeability and contingency of all things?')" (Brinkmann, 2013, p. 6). Pragmatism can help researchers escape modernist norms, not through a postmodern dismissal and deconstruction of all practices but through a practical engagement in ongoing cycles of reflection and action.

2.4 Agential realism.

Technocratic research is based on **representationalism**—the binary belief that there is a firm distinction between representations (words, images, thoughts) and the phenomena (things) they are meant to represent. Educational researchers are likely to assume, for example, that the phenomena being studied exist separate from how researchers perceive or describe them and from any instruments that are designed to measure them. For example, they may use a time-on-task observation protocol to measure "attention" or "student engagement," assuming that the measurement protocol will not interact with the phenomenon being observed, and that any "bias" can be controlled through using valid measurement procedures. Yet the instrument itself is active in producing the phenomenon—in this case, defining engagement as looking at the teacher or assignment.

"Representationalism," Barad (2003) argued, "is so deeply entrenched within Western culture that it has taken on a commonsense appeal. It seems inescapable, if not downright natural" (p. 806). Representationalism feels natural and inevitable primarily because it adheres to many modernist tenets, particularly the Cartesian mind/body binary and its a priori distinction between the observer and the observed, or the internal and external worlds. Yet, as Barad (2003) pointed out, "the 'knower' does not stand in a relation of absolute externality to the natural world being investigated—there is no such exterior observational point. . . . We do not obtain knowledge by standing outside the world; we know because 'we' are *of* the world" (pp. 828–829).

Barad (2007) instead thought about the scientific and social worlds dialectically, opening a third space between these two poles with an approach she called **agential realism:**

> Agential realism rejects the notion of a correspondence relation between words and things and offers in its stead a causal explanation of how discursive practices are related to material phenomena. It does so by shifting the focus from the nature of representations (scientific and other) to the nature of discursive practices (including technoscientific ones). . . . Crucial to this theoretical framework is a strong commitment to accounting for the material nature of practices and how they come to matter. (p. 45)

Barad challenged both the modernist valorization of the physical world and the postmodernist view of the material world as being subservient to language and discourse. Thus, she avoided the limits of pitting modern and postmodern approaches against each other. "The fact that scientific knowledge is constructed [via discourse] does not imply that science does not 'work,' and the fact that science 'works' does not mean that we have discovered human-independent facts about nature" (Barad, 2007, p. 40).

Whereas Barad agreed, in line with Foucault (1972, 1980) and Butler (1993), that subjects have been historically and discursively produced, she did not take the position that words matter more than things. Instead, she thought of words and things dialectically, arguing, for example, that "Foucault does not tell us in what way the biological and historical are 'bound together' such that one is constitutive of the other" (Barad, 2003, p. 809). Accordingly, Barad took a **posthumanist** position to argue that human and nonhuman forces both make agential contributions to phenomena; the discursive and material are entangled and co-constituting.

Barad's posthumanist approach extended Haraway's (1991) examinations of how categories such as human and nonhuman are produced. Barad sought both to blur the human/nonhuman binary and to decenter the human subject. In this way, she challenged the assumption of a sovereign, essentialized individual over the physical, material world. She saw both words and things—the discursive and the material—as active coparticipants in producing the world. As Plauborg (2018) argued, "The nonhuman is also a vital player" (p. 327). The material world of classrooms, for instance—digital screens, buildings, whiteboards, pencils, desks, workbooks, and paper—are all "making constitutive differences to human learning processes. . . . It is . . . a comprehensive apparatus that creates the teaching situation and what becomes agentic depends on the specificities of what is entangled" (Plauborg, 2018, p. 327).

Yet, educational research is often focused on the actions of teachers and students, with only a brief mention of the research setting in the Methodology section; it is rarely part of the findings. Instead of examining how one phenomenon interacts with another to cause an outcome (the traditional notion of causality), Barad (2007) examined how the overlapping agencies of material and discursive practices emerge in relation to each other. "Central to my analysis is the agential realist understanding of matter as a dynamic and shifting entanglement of relations, rather than as a property of things" (p. 35).

In her formulation of agential realism, Barad (2007) derived many concepts from quantum physics, the dominant paradigm in the field of physics for more than a century. For many years, quantum physicists have rejected the classical Newtonian model of a world composed of individual entities, such as atoms, with fixed properties. Quantum mechanics, as articulated in particular by Bohr (1998), suggests that a full and objective understanding of the external, physical world is beyond science's reach because all phenomena change the instant they are observed.

Quantum physicists have observed that light, for example, is both a wave and a particle. It is not inherently one or the other; its properties depend on the apparatus used to measure it. This principle of wave–particle duality suggests that phenomena do not have specific properties or even necessarily exist until they are measured. The process of observation alters any phenomenon, and there is no possibility to understand the nature of phenomena free from the influences of observation processes.

Similarly, any indicator or statistical measure breaks down once it becomes a target used for evaluation purposes (Goodhart, 1975). When a teacher knows, for example, that their performance evaluation is based on the thoroughness of their instruction, measured by how many chapters they cover, they may rush through the material at the expense of covering it thoroughly. Schools often conflate measures with targets, and, as Strathern (1997) argued, "when a measure becomes a target it ceases to become a good measure" (p. 308). Different forms of observation or evaluation will result in different observed outcomes of what were thought to be the same phenomena. The many technocratic research regimes that are meant to assure objectivity, neutrality, and freedom from bias, then, inevitably fail.

Bohr asserted that it is impossible to separate a phenomenon from the apparatus used to measure it. For example, when teachers observe students' reading by measuring their speed and fluency to determine a grade-level score, they generate reader identities such as "above," "below," or "at" grade level. Yet if reading is assessed in another way—for instance, in terms of reading comprehension through illustration or role-play—then the findings generated may be different or even inverted from what the earlier measurement has produced. Student reading capacities and experiences may differ, then, depending on the observation and measurement procedures used. While many educational researchers would argue from a representationalist perspective that there is a "true" version of a student's reading level that exists "out there," from agential realist perspective, a student's reading level exists only via what is measured—and this reading level may change according to the means of measurement.

Barad (2007) contended that objects and agencies of observation are **entangled**; they are inseparable, and each is constitutive of the other. She applied Bohr to reject the classical idea that physical reality is composed of external, independent entities or objects that researchers can identify and measure. "For Bohr, phenomena—entanglements of objects and agencies of observation—constitute physical reality; phenomena (not independent objects) are the objective referent of measured properties" (Barad, 2007, p. 309). This echoes Marx's idea that the smallest unit of analysis is a relation rather than an individual.

Quantum physics suggests that even time and space do not exist as "determinate givens outside of phenomena" (Barad, 2007, p. 315). Space and time are themselves—entangled with processes of observation. They are not passive or bounded entities that exist apart from observers. Yet most educational researchers continue to assume that space is a passive, bounded entity and that time runs on a fixed linear course. Teachers are likely to believe that student learning moves in a continuous, upward curve, where knowledge acquisition is cumulative. The notion that learning is measurable and follows a linear trajectory fits into modernist logic and its metanarrative of progress. Barad argued instead that phenomena such as time and space are neither bounded nor measurable as independent entities. Barad (2007) asserted that space and time are iteratively reworked, enfolded, and performed: "Not even a moment exists on its own. 'This' and 'that,' 'here' and 'now,' don't preexist what happens but come alive with each meeting. The world and its possibilities for becoming are remade with each moment" (p. 396).

In a classroom, for example, the past, present, and future may overlap for students in ways that are counter to teachers' expectations. Teachers may assume that a lesson on fractions begins and ends when the bell rings, yet student learning is always a jumble of what was learned before, what is presented now, and what students expect the teacher will want later. What students encounter tomorrow will also alter how they perceive what they learned in the past. Time and space are constantly reconfiguring. As Juelskjær (2013) explained, "Mattering and materialising are dynamic processes through which temporality and spatiality are produced as something specific" (p. 755). Space and time are dynamic and agential, part of the material-discursive forces at work in producing educational realities.

The continuing reliance on a Newtonian understanding of reality, along with representationalism and other positivist principles, is ironic because technocratic researchers, who rely on a narrative of progress, are basing their work upon an outdated classical physics paradigm that is well over 200 years old. They ignore the possibilities that the contemporary prevailing paradigm—quantum physics—offers. While quantum physics should not become another metanarrative that seeks to explain everything, ideas from this paradigm can help open third spaces, dismantling the artificial line drawn between "scientific" inquiry and "social" educational practice that maintains the elite status of research as a privileged technical activity. This means that research can no longer be conducted outside the bounds of the everyday practice of teachers in schools, as the province of universities, third-party evaluators, and administrators. As Dewey (1929) argued, "No conclusion of scientific research can be converted into an immediate rule of educational art" (p. 9).

References

Barad, K. (2003). Posthumanist performativity: Toward an understanding of how matter comes to matter. *Gender and Science: New Issues, 28*(3), 801–831.

Barad, K. (2007). *Meeting the universe halfway: Quantum physics and the entanglement of matter and meaning*. Duke University Press.

Barthes, R. (1981). The discourse of history. *Comparative Criticism, 3*, 7–20.

Berthold-Bond, D. (1989). *Hegel's grand synthesis: A study of being, thought, and history*. State University of New York Press.

Biesta, G. J. J. (2014). Pragmatising the curriculum: Bringing knowledge back into the curriculum conversation, but via pragmatism. *The Curriculum Journal, 25*(1), 29–49.

Biesta, G. J. J., & Burbules, N. C. (2003). *Pragmatism and educational research*. Rowman and Littlefield Publishers.

Bohr, N. (1998). *The philosophical writings of Niels Bohr, Vol. 4, Causality and Complementarity*. Ox Bow Press.

Brinkmann, S. (2013). *John Dewey: Science for a changing world*. Transaction Publishers.

Butler, J. (1993). Imitation and gender insubordination. In H. Abelove, M. A. Barale, & D. M. Halperin (Eds.), *The lesbian and gay studies reader* (pp. 307–320). Routledge.

Butler, J. (1999). *Gender trouble: Feminism and the subversion of identity*. Routledge.

Butler, J. (2004). *Precarious life: The powers of mourning and violence*. Verso.

Descartes, R. (1967). *The philosophical works of Descartes*. Cambridge University Press.

Dewey, J. (1896). The reflex arc concept in psychology. *The Psychological Review, 3*(4), 357–370.

Dewey, J. (1922). *Human nature and conduct: An introduction to social psychology*. Cosimo.

Dewey, J. (1929). *The later works of John Dewey (1925–1953)*. Southern Illinois University Press.

Foucault, M. (1972). *The archaeology of knowledge and the discourse on language*. Pantheon Books.

Foucault, M. (1973). *The birth of the clinic: An archaeology of medical perception*. Vintage.

Foucault, M. (1977). *Discipline and punish: The birth of the prison*. Pantheon Books.

Foucault, M. (1980). *Power/Knowledge: Selected interviews and other writings, 1972–77*. Pantheon Books.

Foucault, M. (1984). Truth and power. In P. Rabinow (Ed.), *The Foucault reader* (pp. 51–75). Pantheon Books.

Foucault, M. (1988). *Technologies of the self: A seminar with Michel Foucault* (L. H. Martin, H. Gutman, & P. Hutton, Eds.). University of Massachusetts Press.

Foucault, M. (1990). *History of Sexuality, Volumes 1–3*. Vintage Books.

Foucault, M. (2006). *History of madness*. Routledge.

Fraenkel, J., Wallen, N., & Hyun, H. (2012). *How to design and evaluate research in education*. McGraw Hill Education.

Goodhart, C. (1975). Problems of monetary management: The U.K. experience. *Papers in Monetary Economics, 1*. Reserve Bank of Australia.

Grewal, I., & Kaplan, C. (Eds.). (1994). *Scattered hegemonies: Postmodernity and transnational feminist practices*. University of Minnesota Press.

Hall, S. (Ed.). (1996). *Representation: Cultural representations and signifying practices*. Sage Publications.

Hammerberg, D. D. (2004). Technologies of the self in classrooms designed as "learning environments": (Im)possible ways of being in early literacy instruction. In B. M. Baker & K. E. Heyning (Eds.), *Dangerous coagulations? The uses of Foucault in the study of education* (pp. 359–361). Peter Lang.

Haraway, D. (1991). *Simians, cyborgs and women: The reinvention of nature*. Routledge.

James, W. (1907). *Pragmatism: A new name for some old ways of thinking*. Harvard University Press.

Juelskjær, M. (2013). Gendered subjectivities of spacetimematter. *Gender and Education, 25*(6), 754–768.

Lyotard, J. (1999). *The postmodern condition: A report on knowledge*. The University of Minnesota Press.

Marx, K. (1971). *Capital: Vol. I. A critical analysis of capitalist production*. Progress Publishers. (Original work published 1887).

Morgenbesser, S. (1977). *Dewey and his critics: Essays from the Journal of Philosophy*. Hackett Publishing.

Munro, D. J. (1985). *Individualism and holism: Studies in Confucian and Taoist values*. Center for Chinese Studies, University of Michigan.

Needham, J. (1954). *Science and civilization in China: Volume I*. Cambridge University Press.

Nielsen, K. (2016). On defining learning from a social-ontological perspective. In A. Qvortrup, M. Wiberg, G. Christensen, & M. Hansbøl (Eds.), *On the definition of learning* (pp. 141–162). University Press of Southern Denmark.

Ollman, B. (1976). *Alienation: Marx's conception of man in capitalist society* (Vol. 9). Cambridge University Press.

Peng, K., Spencer-Rodgers, J., & Nian, Z. (2006). Naïve dialecticism and the Tao of Chinese thought. In U. Kim, K. S. Yang, & K. K. Hwang (Eds.), *Indigenous and cultural psychology* (pp. 247–262). Springer.

Peters, M. (1999). (Posts-) modernism and structuralism: Affinities and theoretical innovations. *Sociological Research Online, 4*(3), 122–138.

Peters, M., & Besley, A. C. (2006). *Building knowledge cultures: Education and development in the age of knowledge capitalism*. Rowman & Littlefield, Publishers.

Pierce, C. S. (1955). *Philosophical writings*. Dover.

Plauborg, H. (2018). Towards an agential realist concept of learning. *Subjectivity, 11*(4), 322–338.

Rasmussen, M. S. (2016). Learning from a social practice theoretical perspective. In A. Qvortrup, M. Wiberg, G. Christensen, & M. Hansbøl (Eds.), *On the definition of learning* (pp. 229–244). University Press of Southern Denmark.

Rorty, R. (1991). *Objectivity, relativism, and truth: Philosophical papers*. Cambridge University Press.

Stallybrass, P., & White, A. (1986). *The politics and poetics of transgression*. Cornell University Press.

Strathern, M. (1997). 'Improving ratings': Audit in the British university system. *European Review, 5*(3), 305–321.

Sullivan, N. (2003). *A critical introduction to queer theory*. New York University Press.

Toulmin, S. (1990). *Cosmopolis: The hidden agenda of modernity*. The University of Chicago Press.

Webb, H. (2012). The splendid and the savage: The dance of opposites in indigenous Andean thought. *Journal of Transpersonal Psychology, 4*(1), 69–83.

THREE

Critiquing Standard Research Methods

IN NEARLY EVERY UNIVERSITY SOCIAL science and education department, graduate students are required to take a research methodology course that covers the skills considered necessary to conduct original research, such as sampling procedures, instrumentation, descriptive and inferential statistics, coding, ethical codes of conduct. These skills are discussed and categorized in terms of two presumed kinds of research: "quantitative" and "qualitative." Quantitative and qualitative research each represent heterogeneous approaches that often overlap in practice, but they are consistently presented as discrete opposites. This artificial division reifies and reduces research methods, which are typically so idealized and decontextualized that students are left confused and frustrated when they set out to apply them. This binary also narrows possibilities for research, privileging quantitative data and methods as more "objective" and "scientific."

Research methods courses are often little more than vocabulary lessons, in which professors define the key methods for each stage of research, invariably presented in a linear sequence:

1. Developing the research question
2. Reviewing the literature
3. Defining research variables
4. Selecting or developing instruments
5. Obtaining ethics review board approval
6. Sampling
7. Collecting data
8. Analyzing data
9. Reporting findings

Research methods texts assume that research will always proceed in this order and that the methods presented for each stage will universally apply to any research setting. They presume that sampling or coding methods, for example, are context-independent tools that can be used in any context. Yet, as Brinkmann (2013) argued, it is "impossible to discover or learn a . . . method in isolation from the subjects and real situations in which we experience these subjects. It is instead necessary to involve concrete phenomena" (p. 164). Or as Dewey (1916) wrote, "There can be no discovery of a method without cases to be studied" (p. 168).

Although research methods courses try to offer universally applicable recipes for how to conduct research, students often leave the courses feeling unprepared. As Tanggaard (2013) wrote,

> With methods books and courses offering a relatively easy, fast-food approach to the world of science, there is . . . a real risk of compartmentalization of research into easily digestible bit(e)s, not lasting long. . . . Meanwhile, the content, or the craft of research tends to slip away. (p. 411)

Students discover that, as Nielsen (1999) described,

> "Doing research in the field [is] much more complicated than described in methodological textbooks. (p. 229)

There is little correspondence between textbook research methods and research practices in the field, though research methodology professors perpetuate and defend their idealized and preferred methods. Conformity to existing ideologies and institutional expectations occurs not because the methods serve researchers particularly well but because researchers were trained and socialized into particular paradigms, and adherence to them protects their careers and justifies resources offered by funders to conduct approved forms of investigation. Governments and philanthropists often state specifically that they will fund only "rigorous," scientifically based research that includes experimental or quasi-experimental studies with empirically testable hypotheses, comparison groups, and other markers of validity. Researchers gain institutional authority and credibility by adhering to these technocratic research methods.

3.1 The false binary of quantitative/qualitative research.

The quantitative/qualitative binary defines every aspect of research: philosophy and epistemology, data types, data collection, and analysis. The term **quantitative** refers to numerical forms of data or data collection that measure mathematically how much or to what degree specific phenomena are present. These types of data are generally collected using measurement scales embedded in tests or surveys. In contrast, the term **qualitative** is used to describe non-numerical data (text, dialogue, observations, images, objects, media) and research methods that generate thematic findings through content analysis or various forms of **coding**—a technocratic term that simply means "looking for patterns" (Saldaña, 2015).

Research methodology instructors and textbooks present students with charts that portray each approach as the opposite of the other. There are occasionally cautionary notes that the approaches should not be viewed as "polar opposites or dichotomies" (Creswell, 2012, p. 11). Yet, they are still presented this way and often introduced in misleading two-column charts (see Table 3.1).

Table 3.1 Quantitative/Qualitative Research Comparison Chart

Quantitative	Qualitative
Deductive	Inductive
Objective, unbiased	Subjective, biased
Predetermined research question (or hypothesis)	Emergent research questions
Tests relationships among variables	Explores patterns, does not demonstrate causality among variables
Structured; set structure for reporting data	Unstructured; flexible structure for reporting data
Large sample size	Small sample size
Uses statistical analysis	Uses thematic analysis, coding of texts or images

This binary representation both reifies and reduces kinds of data, methods, and approaches to research. As Allwood (2012) argued,

> The properties found in one or the other of the two columns of lists like this often do not appear to have any necessary connection to one another and it is not difficult to find examples of research methods or approaches of both quantitative and qualitative labeling that include properties from both columns. (p. 1424)

The simplistic and abstract presentation of quantitative/qualitative research reduces and obscures the heterogeneity within each kind of research. The typical idealized presentation, in particular, hides the diversity among qualitative researchers who may vary widely in their approaches to

1. generalizability of results—some claim that they can generalize their results, others do not;
2. quantification—some quantify some of their data, others do not;
3. causal explanations—some believe that qualitative investigations can yield causal explanations, others believe that the best they can achieve is description, without attributing causality; and
4. structure—some investigations (such as discourse analysis) can be tightly structured and narrowly focused—others are holistic and broad, seeking to characterize the gestalt of a research setting. (Allwood, 2012)

The false binary of quantitative/qualitative research also reifies each kind of research, exaggerating differences between them. The two supposedly different forms of research are often, in practice, neither separable nor distinct from each other. A yes/no or multiple-choice question on a survey, for instance, can yield either qualitative or quantitative data. For example, consider a survey question such as When you have free time to yourself, what do you like to do best?

A. Watch TV
B. Use social media
C. Read
D. Spend time outdoors

E. Play video games
F. Other: ______________

Participants' responses to this question are text (a type of data considered qualitative), yet researchers are likely to quantify and analyze these responses mathematically (producing a quantitative measure, such as the percentage of respondents who watch TV). Though the data may be analyzed quantitatively, they are then verbalized in a narrative (qualitative) description. As Vidich and Lyman (1998) argued, "All research methods are at bottom qualitative . . . ; the use of quantitative data or mathematical procedures does not eliminate the intersubjective element that underlies social research" (p. 44).

In the textbook presentation of quantitative and qualitative research, data types and paradigms are frequently conflated. This is rarely acknowledged or made explicit in research courses, leading to confusion among students. Students may assume, for instance, that if they are collecting qualitative data, such as student narratives, then they are doing qualitative research—even when they are testing a hypothesis by tallying a number of specific types of utterances. Conversely, students may design a study employing a qualitative paradigm without a predetermined research question while collecting solely quantitative data (or qualitative data that they quantify).

Although there is seldom acknowledgment of the overlap between quantitative and qualitative types of data or data collection and analysis methods in research methodology textbooks, the texts acknowledge that research studies may use both quantitative and qualitative data or methods. The textbooks refer to these as *mixed method research studies*. In most cases, mixed method research describes studies in which the researcher intends to collect both qualitative and quantitative types of data, for instance assessment scores or survey responses, along with interviews or observations, rather than research that consciously adopts the theoretical frameworks from both underlying paradigms.

In addition to confusing students with its idealization of research practices, the quantitative/qualitative binary upholds the scientistic hierarchy that values quantitative research over qualitative. Students undertake mixed method studies mainly because they are encouraged to graft a quantitative component onto a desired qualitative design to satisfy institutional pressures that privilege quantitative forms. The privileging of quantitative research means that even when researchers are collecting only qualitative data, they are still encouraged to adopt quantitative methods.

Feeling pressured to mirror the scientistic pretensions of quantitative research, qualitative researchers have developed a series of technical-sounding terms (*in vivo coding, process coding, descriptive coding, values coding, analytic memos*) to legitimate the interpretive process of looking for patterns and sorting data into categories. Even critical ethnographers often feel that they must validate their work by adopting research methods from quantitative paradigms promoted by institutions or funders. Through **triangulation** or offering additional quantitative measures that reinforce qualitative findings, researchers and students are assured that their findings will be more credible and well received.

The gate-keeping institutions at universities, such as admissions committees and institutional review boards, privilege quantitative studies that fit institutional norms. As one professor at a European university cautioned a potential doctoral student from the United States after reading their research proposal draft, "They [the admissions committee members] don't believe in what you do. You need to add statistics, they believe in statistics. They think if the numbers say it, then it is true. They've bought all the positivist stuff" (personal communication, October 13, 2014). Even after the student revised the proposed comparative ethnographic study, adding quantitative measures—surveys and test scores—to conduct a mixed method comparative study to investigate special education in two countries, the professor wrote the following:

> Thank you for sending me your proposal. I think it has improved, however, it might still be too complicated for my colleagues in the committee. Remember that they are classical positivistic trained, so if you can make it more explicit and more simple, it improves your chances. . . . You have a really interesting topic. It's important, but it's not what they are looking for. They want clear-cut studies with clear variables you can compare. (personal communication, April 3, 2015)

The insistence on isolating and simplifying variables to make them measurable (and thus "researchable") effectively requires researchers to dumb down their initial ideas and stifles attempts to take up complex social factors in changing environments.

To increase chances of acceptance, the same professor went on to suggest that the student introduce a simplistic binary to the study:

> I agree with [my colleague] that it would help you to make the U.S. school "the good example" central for your proposal. The logic of the proposal would then be something like: "We are having a problem here in [our country] with inclusion. At some schools (that are comparable to our schools) in the U.S., they are doing a great job including the students (this needs to be documented). I would like to do a case research study about what they are doing." I think this logic would be understandable to my colleagues. You will then need to give more details in the text about the good example school from the U.S. (personal communication, April 3, 2015)

Though this advice contradicted the prior experience of the prospective student and ran counter to the professor's own philosophical approach (to conduct open-ended, critical ethnographies rather than hypothesis-driven comparative studies), the professor felt it was necessary to adapt the study to conform to the normative institutional narrative, which positioned the U.S. educational system as a superior model. As exemplified here, local institutional norms can mandate reproducing the biased social norms that student studies may seek to challenge.

In addition to the explicit forms of advice that students may receive from university research advisors, there are other implicit ways that institutions privilege technocratic research proposals. When researchers review sample lists of successful or funded research proposals, for example, they may find that they are all quantitative or mixed method studies, effectively discouraging submissions of open-ended or qualitative studies. In the United States, federal guidelines for funded educational research suggested that researchers should seek

> information to identify, plan, and implement . . . programs and practices that have been proved to be effective through scientifically based research . . . which is defined as having six specific components: use empirical methods, involve rigorous and adequate data analysis, rely on measurements that provide valid and reliable data, use either an experimental or quasi-experimental design, allow for replicability, undergo expert scrutiny. (U.S. Department of Education, 2018)

Beyond the confusion and normalizing pressure generated by the false binary dividing qualitative from quantitative research methods, the binary also limits the development of new research methods. "Researchers who believe that it is only allowable to develop new methods *within* the assumed reference frames of each of the qualitative and quantitative approaches will miss opportunities for fruitful combinations of features belonging to both of the approaches" (Allwood, 2012, p. 1427). Ultimately, the distinction drawn between qualitative and quantitative research is "problematic and of limited value." It is more useful, Allwood (2012) argued, to look at the "pros and cons of research methods . . . in relation to the specific research context that they are used in (including the research question posed and the resources available for the research) and not on a general abstract level" (p. 1418).

3.2 Rethinking "researchable" questions and variables.

Universities and other research organizations privilege certain kinds of research questions and hypotheses—those considered most appropriate by dominant research discourse. Researchers are encouraged to measure phenomena that are readily identifiable and easy to operationalize in practice. Institutional pressure and researcher socialization lead to overreliance on existing variables with a history in the literature and on already validated instruments (surveys, test, questionnaires, observation protocols). These institutional pressures narrow possible lines of action that researchers can take.

The first step of the normative study design process is to generate a research question. Methods textbooks distill this into an abstract procedure and make claims, for instance, that "good research questions possess four essential characteristics"; they must be feasible, clear, significant, and ethical (Fraenkel et al., 2012, p. 28). Such abstractions assume that these are static, objective, value-free determinations, rather than always contingent, context-dependent, and in flux.

In the field of education, acceptable research questions are seen scientistically as those that ask about the relationships between one or more variables while specifying measurable educational outcomes. Students are expected to write research questions so that hypotheses may be generated from them. A hypothesis is supposed to propose an explanation for a phenomenon that involves a relationship between two variables, and it must be testable. In the study design process, students are asked to write up a section on expected findings, often even when they wish to adopt **grounded theory** or an open-ended ethnographic approach.

Scientistic research questions that seek to investigate hypotheses have the goal of *explanation*, yet this is only one type of research approach. Research questions that have the goal of *understanding* are rarely accepted in the field of education. Open-ended research questions that ask, for example, "What are the patterns of X?" or "How does community Y interpret a particular phenomenon?" are rejected. Although students may be interested in understanding the impact of discipline policy changes in their schools, research advisors who follow a technocratic paradigm rarely accept this kind of general inquiry. They generally reject the phenomenological goal of understanding, and they instead insist that students rewrite their questions in a way that operationalizes them and leads to a causal explanation.

Technocratic norms force students to simplify their ideas and write "researchable" questions that they can measure, such as "How does X change in school policy impact suspension rates for Y group of students?" This reductive process narrows the focus of students' investigations and prevents them from studying—and trying to understand—the topics they were originally interested in or that were grounded in their experience. The definition of a researchable question directs the "content of science through constraining problem-choice or through requiring . . . particular kinds of theoretical and experimental formulation" (Dear, 1991, p. 5). What counts as a researchable question from a technocratic perspective also discourages exploratory research that is intended to discover indeterminate or unknown problems, or more complex studies that investigate multiple, changing variables.

There is an epistemological difference between the goal of explanation, which is characteristic of technocratic science, and the goal of understanding, which reflects phenomenological approaches. Hermeneutic thinkers such as Gadamer (1976) and Habermas (1971) assert that the social sciences cannot conform to the logic of the natural sciences. Weber (2011), too, urged that the social sciences are meant to understand social phenomena in terms of meaningful categories of human experience and that the approach of the natural sciences is not applicable to social inquiry. The task of the social sciences, in a phenomenological view, should be to develop deeper understanding—not simply to build explanations based on general laws and theories, as is the case with natural science. The goal of social sciences, they argue, should be to interpret social action in terms of cultural assumptions and intersubjective intentions. This interpretive dimension cannot rely on observation and explanation alone but must include analysis of the complex meanings of social practices (Apel, 1984).

Ignoring this critique and following technocratic norms, research advisors insist that any phenomenon students wish to investigate must be turned into a measurable variable. Even when students wish to take a critical stance and conduct an ethnography or another form of research that is based on the idea that themes should emerge during the course of study, research advisors often inappropriately require students to submit operational definitions in their proposals.

Common variables measured in the field of education may include instructional techniques, type of curriculum, gender, ethnicity, socioeconomic background, student engagement, attendance rates, self-esteem, learning styles, parent education level, and so forth. Technocratic researchers believe that they can investigate how variables influence outcomes, and that it is possible to control for all extraneous factors and eliminate bias through adherence to scientistic data collection methods. There is no recognition of how entangled variables are in social relations.

Research methods textbooks further divide variables into an independent/dependent binary. An **independent variable** is seen as a phenomenon that researchers isolate, manipulate, and use to explain a particular effect or outcome. The outcome of the hypothesized impact of the independent variable is called a **dependent variable.** For example, researchers may try to establish a causal link between inadequate nutrition (independent variable) and poor academic performance (dependent variable). This type of link is called a **directional relationship**, meaning that variable A (nutrition) is hypothesized to influence variable B (academic performance). The production of such directional hypotheses often leads to the assumption that there is only a one-way causal relationship. For example, researchers who set out to study the degree to which chronic absence affects test scores may neglect to study how school failure leads to chronic absences.

There is another possible relationship between variables, referred to as a **correlational relationship.** This means that there is a relationship between variables A and B, but it is not possible to establish if one causes the other.

Despite the technocratic assumption that research can and should determine how one variable affects another, causality in social relations always acts in complex ways involving multiple, overlapping variables that go well beyond the two variable types that research methods instructors require students to employ.

To claim that an independent variable (such as a new literacy program) is the causal variable that impacts the dependent variable (such as academic performance), researchers are expected to design studies that have as few differences in the treatment of subjects or conditions of the research setting as possible—other than the independent variable. The goal is to hold constant all factors other than the independent variable. Yet, no research study, regardless of how large its sample size or how robust its methods, will ever be able to conclusively establish cause and effect or to unerringly inform policy. It is not possible to isolate or fully describe any externalized independent variable, such as literacy or classroom management, or any internal state such as student motivation.

Supposed independent/dependent variables, Barad (2007) argued, exist only in and through one another. Phenomena are always in a process of co-constructing each other. For example, race and literacy should not be described reductively in a causal relationship, such as "X race leads to Y literacy outcomes." Race and literacy exist in and through each other. A student does not become a reader isolated from any other identity. "The generation of identities, knowledge, and meaning in racial terms is so salient in the United States," wrote Lave (2019), "that racial meanings are generated both in the presence and absence of ongoing activity" (p. 98).

As Lave (2019) argued further, "Culture produces learning, even as learning always produces culture" (p. 6). It makes no sense, then, to isolate variables and determine how X affects Y or any other causal relationship. Instead, taking relations as the smallest unit of analysis, as Marx (1887/1971) suggested, enables recognition of the ways that phenomena are entangled and expands possible research directions.

The insistence on determining independent/dependent variables requires educational researchers to assume that they can measure the effectiveness of a specific curriculum in a way that is disentangled from any other phenomena. They assume that any additional influential factors like individual teacher variation, teacher–student relationships, or content area are irrelevant or controlled. Erickson and Gutierrez (2002) illustrated the difficulty of specifying variables when studying different instructional methods with an example of a quantitative research study that investigated the performance of day care centers based on class size and staff-to-student ratios. The study claimed, in concert with popular belief, that smaller class sizes were preferable. When qualitative researchers followed up on this study, however, they observed that the larger groups always had more than one adult in the room, which led to fewer adult-to-child interactions:

> Staff-to-staff schmoozing was the actual proximal independent variable, not the overall staff-to-student ratio or the size of the groups, in and of themselves . . . at issue was . . . the specific interactive use of such potential resources within the conduct of instructional practice. (Erickson & Gutierrez, 2002, p. 21)

Even something seemingly as simple and straightforward to measure as staff-to-student ratio turns out to be a complex variable to study. Even the simplest of objects, Dewey argued, "will prove to be heterogeneous, contextual, and complex and will possess a changeable relationship to its environment" (as cited in Brinkmann, 2013, pp. 41–42). Or, as Clifford (1988) said, there are no indivisible, bounded phenomena or "pure products."

In a further attempt to bracket out variables, research methodology texts divide variables into a continuous/categorical binary. **Continuous variables** refer to factors that are measured and ranked in quantitative terms on a scale. Topics like anxiety level or reading fluency are usually treated as continuous variables; they are quantified with imposed scale levels that are presumed to show regularized degrees of variation. Other phenomena such as gender, ethnicity, and teaching methods are termed **categorical variables**. They are viewed as discrete, either/or phenomena that cannot be measured on scales because they are thought to be distinct from each other and homogeneous within each category.

Yet determining whether a variable is continuous or categorical is not a neutral task. Fraenkel et al. (2012), for instance, critiqued any research that collapses variables like interest or anxiety into categories, arguing that the "dividing line between groups (for example, between individuals of high, middle, or low anxiety) is almost always arbitrary (that is, lacking any defensible rationale)" (p. 80). Fraenkel et al. however, did not question establishing ethnicity or gender as categorical variables. They defined categorical variables as situations where "a person is either in one category or another, not somewhere in between . . . all members within each category of this variable are considered the same" (Fraenkel et al., 2012, pp. 78–79). Yet when authors of research method texts assume categories like male/female, White/Black/Latinx, or heterosexual/homosexual are stable and easily assigned, they disregard hybrid categories and self-ascribed labels, including nonbinary, transgender, and intersectional identities of various communities (Crenshaw, 1991), and they ignore how students blend and shift between socially drawn categories (Pollock, 2005).

Pollock's (2005) research offers an illustration of how racial boundaries were both enacted and disrupted by students in one California high school. The students in her study constantly adopted, shifted, and discarded the race categories imposed by the school. They often did this for strategic reasons—to affiliate with a group of peers or to maximize chances of getting into a particular school that had race-based admission quotas. They also played guessing games and invented new categories, combining, for example, Japanese and Filipino to create a new term ("Japapino"). Their play demonstrates recognition that race is not fixed or an immutable fact of nature. Pollock termed this "race-bending." The construction of new racial categories has occurred throughout history, as Katzew (1996) documented in her work on Spanish colonial casta paintings. These paintings were commissioned in colonial Mexico in the 17th century to produce a hierarchy of relations among colonists as they mixed with various Indigenous and African slave populations. The history of casta paintings illustrates the ways that race has always been fluid, though it continues to be described in social science research as a static, independent, categorical variable.

Defining racial and cultural identities categorically can further impose a false homogenization on social groups. When educational researchers, for example, study Latinx students as a single categorical group, they ignore all the differences within communities, such as national origin, class, proximity to border, gradations of skin color, languages spoken (Spanish or Indigenous languages), or other factors that establish hierarchies of power and privilege. These hierarchies can exist even within a single family, as one sixth grader described:

> My mother is brown-skinned and I am of a lighter skin tone. They call me "White Chocolate" and my brother "Café con Leche." They [my friends] say I don't fit with this group and I say, "No, I'm Latino" . . . They are just jealous of my skin tone. They want to be that color because that color gets more privileges like to get into college, they like people more. (Blakely, 2007, p. 116)

Heterogeneity within communities can be even more intense than the differences between the racialized communities that schools refer to in policy and practice. When researchers define variables using dominant methodologies, they reify and reduce complexities of gender, ethnicity, class, and other socially drawn categories of identity, oversimplifying the identities of their subjects.

In addition to treating class, race, and gender identities as homogenous categorical variables, educational researchers commonly treat instructional methods as categorical. Researchers may measure the learning outcomes of different curriculum packages or instructional strategies. Thompson and Mackiewicz (2014), for example, looked at what writing tutors say during a tutoring session and divided utterances into categorical variables—questions versus statements. They concluded that question-asking, especially open-ended questions, is more likely to keep students engaged than making statements. Yet looking simplistically at the data (number of questions versus statements) does not necessarily reflect a tutor's capacity to engage a student. A statement such as "Tell me more about what you meant here" is likely to solicit more from the student than a question such as, "How could you make this clearer?" Though this question is open-ended, it embeds the tutor's evaluation that the writing is confusing, and it directs the student to come up with different wording without offering any scaffolding or support. While the researchers coded these utterances as statements versus questions, in the discourse one may operate more like the other—a question may shut down the student–tutor dialogue, whereas a statement may open it up.

Educational researchers continue to try to isolate variables to measure, yet as Dewey (1896) argued, "The material is too great in mass and too varied in style to fit into existing pigeon-holes, and the cabinets of science break of their own dead weight" (p. 357). Isolating and operationalizing variables will always be problematic because this requires phenomena to have a fixed, static meaning, whereas classrooms and communities are in constant flux.

3.3 Instrumentation and problems with validity and reliability.

Researchers who design studies adhering to fixed social science methods assume that they can control any extraneous variables to generate valid and reliable research with findings that any other researcher should be able to replicate. Given the fluid, ever-changing nature of social relations, great amounts of time and effort are misspent on developing methods that promise reliability and validity. Yet, as a part of neoliberal standards-based education, researchers are required to focus on replicability and generalizability to receive government funding. As the U.S. Department of Education's (2018) *Guidelines for Education Research and Development* stated,

> In order to build a coherent body of work to inform evidence-based decision making, there is a need to increase the visibility and value of reproducibility and replication studies among education research stakeholders. Efforts to reproduce and replicate research findings are central to the accumulation of scientific knowledge that helps inform evidence-based decision making and policies. (p. 1)

The goal of designing valid and reliable research studies is rarely questioned in the field. Yet this misguided aim leads to the unquestioning maintenance of educational norms that consistently produce inequity.

To be considered valid, researchers must demonstrate that their studies are actually measuring the phenomena they claim to be studying, and that the findings can be generalized. Research methods texts describe at least two kinds of validity—**internal validity** (the study measures what it claims to measure, and not some other phenomena) and **external validity** (findings are generalizable to other similar populations). Some texts go further, claiming that researchers should address other imagined forms of internal validity: content validity, criterion validity, and construct validity. Research methods texts, for example, give an example of content validity as "whether the scores from the instrument show that the test's content relates to what the test is intended to measure" (Creswell, 2012, p. 162). Construct validity is further specified circularly as "the validity of inferences about the constructs (or variables) in the study" (Creswell, 2012, p. 303). These kinds of definitions create an elitist language of research; they are opaque and difficult to apply in practice, and they are unlikely to lead to a substantive critique of the usefulness of a study's instruments.

Most research textbooks claim that any "threats to internal validity" can be eliminated or controlled. As one research methods textbook stated, the goal in designing a study is

> to design them so that the inferences you draw are true or correct. Threats to drawing these correct inferences need to be addressed. . . . Threats to validity refer to specific reasons for why we can be wrong when we make an inference in an experiment because of covariance, causation, constructs, or whether the causal relationship holds over variations in persons, setting, treatments, and outcomes. (Creswell, 2012, p. 303)

To control for all the potentially influential factors in a study would amount to removing research subjects from themselves and any context, as if students were blank slates and classrooms were sanitized laboratories.

The idea that threats to internal validity can be eliminated or controlled may be useful in the hard sciences, but not in schools. As Erickson and Gutierrez (2002) argued,

> Educational treatments are situated and dynamically interactive. They are locally constructed social ways of life involving continual monitoring and mutual adjustment among persons, not relatively replicable entities like chemical compounds or surgical procedures or hybrid seed corn or manufactured airplane wings. High fidelity implementation is rare in education—for reasons of local exigency—and despite the accountability pressures and the wishes of experimenters to avoid this major threat to internal validity, there are real-world limits on how "faithful" the implementation will be of even the most structured of instructional programs. (p. 21)

Despite the ever-changing conditions of learning in classrooms, educational researchers are required to ensure the **reliability** of their studies' findings. To be considered reliable, a study must be able to produce repeatedly the same findings in any supposedly similar setting. Technocratic researchers believe that there are three types of such consistency: over time (test–retest reliability), across items (internal reliability), and across different researchers (interrater reliability). Educators are trained to believe that any instrument used in a study (observation protocol, interview schedule, survey, or assessment) will yield the same results if repeated with the same subjects at a later time, or the same results regardless of which researcher does the observation or scoring (interrater reliability). Research methods courses idealize the notion of reliability and ignore the impossibility of attaining it in practice.

Critical reflection in research methodology courses is usually limited to debating how terms such as validity and reliability apply to qualitative versus quantitative research. Research methods instructors, assuming that qualitative methods are inherently different from quantitative methods, argue that alternative frameworks for establishing validity and reliability are appropriate and achievable. Agreeing that qualitative researchers cannot be expected to match the controlled laboratory conditions of other scientific research, Lincoln and Guba (1985) offered alternative criteria for establishing validity and reliability for qualitative researchers: truth value, applicability, and consistency. This approach, however, simply renames technocratic constructs—internal and external validity and reliability—without any further critique of their appropriateness or the likelihood that they will help produce more rigorous research.

The privileging of the constructs of validity and reliability contributes to the normalization of educational discourse and maintenance of the status quo. Many commonly measured variables (self-esteem, student engagement, or level of parent education) may have multiple instruments that are already validated and available for researchers to use in their own research studies, and there is an implied preference for using such instruments. Research advisors often insist that students use these instruments to make their studies seem more valid rather than designing their own observation protocols, tests, or other measures. Using previously developed instruments supports a type of validity called **concurrent validity**. This practice is said to enable researchers to piggyback on the validity claims already established for the instrument by prior researchers.

A common source that researchers and students are told to consult to find already validated instruments is the Buros Mental Measurements Yearbook (MMY). First published in 1938 and updated every three years, the yearbook is viewed as the state-of-the-art standard for valid psychological and educational measurement tools. As the Buros website noted,

> The MMY includes timely, consumer-oriented test reviews, providing evaluative information to promote and encourage informed test selection. . . . To be

> reviewed in the MMY a test must be commercially available, be published in the English language, and be new, revised, or widely used since it last appeared in the MMY series. . . . Tests also must include sufficient documentation supporting their technical quality to meet criteria for review. (Carlson et al., 2020)

The MMY amounts to a narrow form of certification for existing quantitative measurement tools—similar to the accreditation of teacher education programs. When researchers limit themselves only to those tools that appear in the MMY, they replicate a technocratic paradigm that reproduces existing problems of epistemology and equity while failing to broaden research possibilities.

When technocratic researchers assume that validated instruments are universal and can be employed in any study, they create a self-referential closed loop. For example, in one quantitative instrument developed to measure student engagement, called the *Behavioral Engagement Related to Instruction* protocol, an engaged student was operationalized as one who "is listening to lecture. Eye contact is focused on the instructor or activity" (Lane & Harris, 2015, p. 85). A disengaged student was defined, in contrast, as unresponsive: "Eyes are closed or not focused on instructor or lecture material" (Lane & Harris, 2015, p. 85). This instrument relies on the underlying metaphor that "paying attention is looking at" (Lakoff & Johnson, 1980). Yet this notion may run counter to students' cultural norms that require them to look away in deference to adults and authority figures such as teachers. What are seen as engaged behaviors also may simply be signs of students "satisficing" or attempting to appear active to please teachers or avoid punishment (Holzkamp, 2013). Many students who appear active may not be paying any attention to the content of the lesson but rather are performing actions so they will be viewed as "ready to learn."

Even an instrument as simple and straightforward as a tally of the materials in a classroom can be misleading if the results are used for comparisons without further context. Measuring the number of books, for example, in various classrooms may not reflect differences in student engagement with reading materials. In one classroom, for example, there may be 250 books on the shelves, whereas in another there are only 12. Though fewer in number, these books may have been purposefully selected based on the current theme and circulate constantly, while the books in the other classroom may remain on the shelf, as they are too difficult for the current students to read—leftovers from when the teacher taught a different grade level. Tools used to measure learning (quizzes, observation protocols, behavior charts, teaching scales) do not always perform as they are meant to do—to measure a skill or independent variable that exists outside the measurement technique itself. "Rather, the instrument produces that technique and alters it" (as cited in Juelskjær & Schwennesen, 2012, p. 11). With any measuring apparatus, certain properties become fixed while others are excluded. Those properties that are normalized through measurement are governed not only by the interests or intent of the researcher but also by the instrument.

Instruments are not, then, passive tools of observation. They create differences and they produce specific phenomena. The apparatuses employed to measure learning (photographs, audio or film recordings, observation notes, surveys, tests) are generally considered material objects. Yet researchers should not assume that any material way of capturing a moment, even a photograph, is a singularly true representation of the world "out there" as it really is. Lenz Taguchi (2010) explained that

> the photograph should not be understood as a representation of the world and what is photographed. Rather, being a part of the pedagogical documentation, it constitutes a constructed cut of an event taking place in a pedagogical space. . . . Since any event is both material and discursive at the same time, the limits of our discursive understandings constitute a constraint on what is possible. . . . As a consequence . . . we are, as educational practitioners, entangled with our observations and documentation—our apparatuses of knowing. (pp. 67–69)

Photographs, observation protocols, surveys, standardized tests, and other instruments commonly used in classrooms to document learning are, as Barad (2007) would say, agential. These instruments contribute to the production of phenomena, and they enact the boundaries that divide one phenomenon from another. As Juelskjær (2013) argued, instruments are "transformative arrangements, enacting what comes to matter" (p. 756). Standardized tests, for example, produce not only student identities of success or failure but also what counts as legitimate knowledge in a given field.

The goal of trying to design valid and reliable studies is pointless given the entanglement of learning and social relations in constantly changing contexts.

Seeing relations as the irreducible minimum for all units in social science research, as Marx (1887/1971) suggested, means understanding each variable (technique, social factor, treatment) as a relation, "containing in themselves, as integral elements of what they are, those parts with which we tend to see them externally tied" (Ollman, 1976, p. 14). As Roeper concluded, "The only instrument complex enough to understand a human being is another human being." (Beneventi, 2016, p. 257)

3.4 Institutional review boards and the cursory administrative determination of ethical practices.

In the standard mandated study design process, after researchers determine their research question, the variables they intend to measure, and the instruments they will use to collect the data, they must submit their proposed study design to their institution's ethical review board. Institutional review boards (IRBs), also known as independent ethics committees, ethical review boards, or research ethics boards, review all proposed research studies that involve human subjects to ensure that they are in accordance with governmental, institutional, and other ethical guidelines. In their cursory administrative evaluations, IRBs reify and reinforce an "ethical/unethical" binary, following a rigid model of ethical absolutism that fails to support researchers in resolving the ongoing ethical dilemmas they face doing research.

In practice, the main objective of IRBs has become risk management—to protect the university or institution from lawsuits or defunding. Bureaucratic needs are primary; ethical concerns are secondary. Resolving ethical dilemmas is not "amenable to prospective review, to an abstract calculation of risks and benefits, and to consent. The problem with IRBs," argued Bosk and De Vries (2004), ". . . is that they are such a distraction from the real difficulties that we face and from the real ethical dilemmas that confront us that we may not recognize and discuss the serious and elemental because we are so busy with the procedural and bureaucratic" (p. 260). University requirements for ethics training rarely, if ever, offer opportunities for students to examine complex, situation-specific ethical dilemmas that occur throughout the research process. IRB review reduces ethical decision-making to a one-time event that happens only in the study's design phase.

The ethics requirement is met in many U.S. universities via simplistic online courses that are completed in a few hours. Once completing the online course, students are issued a document that certifies them as "ethical researchers." Most methodology courses include a single lecture on ethics, and textbooks contain a single chapter on the topic, with little to no integration of ethical issues in other chapters. In this brief exposure, students are primarily provided with generic secondary source materials. The textbooks may include a short summary of the Tuskegee syphilis experiment, a clinical study conducted from 1932 to 1972 on African American men by the U.S. Public Health Service that misled patients, denying them the treatment they thought they were receiving. Apart from this common historical reference, ethical discussion and activities are abstract. Standard research methods texts offer only decontextualized lists of dos and don'ts based on a rigid ethical/unethical binary. These lists imply that all ethical obligations will be met if researchers simply check off each item, from obtaining informed consent to maintaining confidentiality, anonymity, nontraceability, and so on.

IRBs insist unilaterally that researchers obtain informed consent. They are required to collect signatures from research subjects, certifying that they understand and agree to the conditions of the study in which they are being asked to participate. Standardized templates for the letters sent to obtain informed consent typically include an introduction or description of the research, purpose of the study, type of research intervention, selection of participants, duration, risks and discomforts, benefits, cautionary notes about confidentiality or privacy, discussion of how findings will be shared or where they will be published, a note on participants' rights to withdraw, and contact information. Yet, as Marzano (2007) argued,

> The prior certification of ethical correctness, like that of informed consent, is in many respects a myth. It . . . enables researchers to resolve by means of a bureaucratic procedure the ethical problems inevitably caused by their presence in the setting and to protect themselves against attempts to attack the moral legitimacy of their work or contest its results. (p. 427)

In the informed consent process, there is a false dichotomy in the idealized line drawn between participants and nonparticipants. The assumption made by IRBs that the term *participants* is a clear and bounded category encourages the neglect of sociospatial relations and networks. When conducting research in a busy social space, there will undoubtedly be "unanticipated situations where people are observed and engaged without full knowledge of the researcher's identity" (Deuchar, 2015, p. 5). Marzano (2007) argued that "it is in fact impossible for all participants to be equally knowledgeable about the research project. . . . It is highly likely that there instead exists a 'hierarchy of consent'" (p. 427). IRBs, however, do not address any possible gray areas in their enforcement of an ethical/unethical binary.

The consent requirements proposed universally by IRBs may also be, in many contexts, entirely inappropriate. In the most extreme example, for instance, IRBs have directed researchers to ask for written consent from illiterate participants. IRB requirements lead researchers to choose primarily convenient settings, where there is established trust in institutions, familiarity with formal or legalistic language, and higher levels of literacy. The prescriptions of ethics committees for upfront written consent leads to the silencing or underrepresentation of marginalized groups, who may be wary of institutional practices.

The dominant binary conception of ethics in IRBs relies on the modernist conception of a static world in which there are "unchangeable goals or an overarching moral regulation under which all people should live at all times" (Brinkmann, 2013, p. 17). The idea that morals are absolute is derived from Kant and other Western Enlightenment thinkers. Kant claimed that moral laws were implanted by God and their presence within us is the only reliable evidence of God's existence (Noddings, 2010). Marx challenged this moral absolutism, arguing that concepts, such as "good," "right," and "just" derive their meaning from context, in relation to the corresponding interests of those who use them. Ollman (1976) argued,

> The very notion that it is logically permissible to take any attitude toward a given "fact" is itself a judgment inherent in the circumstances out of which it emerges. Rather than being logically independent of what it is, any choice—as well as the idea that one has a choice—is linked by innumerable threads to the real world, including the life, class interest, and character of the person acting. (pp. 45–46)

Tuhiwai Smith (1999) argued further that "the social 'good' against which ethical standards are determined" is based on "the Western sense of the individual and of individualized property. . . . Community and Indigenous rights or views in this area are generally not recognized and not respected" (p. 118).

Ignoring or dismissing any critiques of moral absolutism, IRBs base their work on the flawed assumptions that researchers can act autonomously, decontextualize ethical concerns, pursue a linear research plan, and follow prescribed methods to attain a clearly stated goal of an unquestioned social "good." Dewey (1891), in contrast, argued that researchers rarely know precisely what their goal is—and, even more rarely, what it should be. He refused to name what is ethically desirable, arguing that there can be no simple recipe or easy answer. He rejected any universal value in ethics and any absolute goal. Dewey maintained that it is not possible for a single theory of morality to apply to lived experience. It is an error, he said, to consider moral theory as a "type of cookbook or as a "collection of rules for conduct." A moral theory cannot be such a thing, for the actions and practices that are the objects of moral deliberation are always particular and determined by context" (as cited in Brinkmann, 2013, p. 117). Dewey asserted that it is necessary to discard traditional, abstract entities such as justice and truth and instead "understand them adverbially, that is, as a means of acting in particular situations, of acting truly, justly" (Brinkmann, 2013, p. 118).

The idea that IRB requirements will "get right the vexing question of how to assure the proper ethical conduct . . . through organizational oversight is a symbol and symptom of a deep misunderstanding . . . and an even deeper misapprehension about how [social science research] conduct is effectively regulated" (Bosk & De Vries, 2004, p. 25). IRBs assume that each researcher can make a choice about what is right or wrong ahead of time. For example, in one ethics lecture slideshow, which accompanies a widely used research methods text, students were instructed to follow this step-by-step procedure:

1. Thank the participants.
2. Ensure that participants do not leave the research more humiliated, insecure, and alienated than when they arrived.
3. Consider the effects on the participants when writing the report and publishing material.
4. Ensure that the researchers have sufficient competence to undertake the research. (Cohen et al., 2011, p. 19)

Ensuring that participants do not leave the research more humiliated, insecure, or alienated is not as easy as ensuring that all participants are thanked, yet major ethical dilemmas are generally regarded with this kind of checklist superficiality.

The current bureaucratic ethics regimes are inadequate and ill-equipped to help researchers develop and refine how to conduct research ethically. The changes to research proposals that IRBs request often amount to little more than petty editing. For example, in an email response to a graduate student's research proposal, IRB staff responded that the student had to change the following:

- In the Questions section of the Consent Document, please identify your advisor as Professor rather than Dr.
- In the Participation in the Research is Voluntary section of the Consent Document, please remove the word "tape-recorded" and replace with "audio-recorded." (personal communication, July 3, 2019)

Research ethics for the social sciences are further based on rules established for biomedical and clinical research. This reflects the modernist privileging of the hard sciences. Many scientistic research aims, such as the preference to draw research subjects from large random samples, are imposed on educational research even though some of the most influential research in the field is based on unrepresentative sample sizes, often as small as one. Piaget (1951), for example, developed his theories of child development from observations of his own child. Though foundational and still widely cited, Piaget's research would not be considered valid, reliable, or ethical in most research institutions today, where controlled experimental studies are privileged at the expense of more complex or nuanced research.

Due to the privileging of quantitative experimental designs, IRB staff are, in general, poorly versed in and dismissive of qualitative research and critical social science or humanities frameworks. Review panels that develop requirements for IRBs have similarly skewed representation, with few qualitative researchers or representatives from critical branches of the social sciences or the humanities (Bosk & De Vries, 2004). Along with lacking discipline-specific knowledge, IRBs often overreach their mandate and violate academic freedom, critiquing entire research designs rather than focusing on their potential harm to subjects. As one IRB chair wrote in a review of a graduate student's research proposal,

> If the sample of four teachers and four educators is analyzed as 'final' interview data, how will that sample size adequately represent a diverse set of viewpoints related to the research questions? If all the convenience sample as well as 'snowball' sample comes from the same institution, then will there be a limitation in the study design? How will you design the sampling of representative viewpoints? Is there an analysis of the appropriate sample size for a 'final' sample of teachers and educators in order to achieve 'saturation' of the thematic analysis? (personal communication, August 15, 2019)

Whether or not the number of interviews the student conducts is representative has nothing to do with evaluating the possibility that the study participants will come to harm during the interview process.

Since IRB members are generally more familiar with quantitative than qualitative approaches to research, they often insist that students adopt technocratic methods. As another IRB chair stated in a message to a graduate student,

> The Committee recognizes that the overall risk to participants in this research is minimal. However, the Committee is concerned that your research design does not include a control group as a basis for comparison of your results. It is unclear how you will answer your research questions without the use of a control group. (personal communication, December 23, 2013)

From their position of authority, IRBs have outsized power to exert a normalizing pressure on researchers that often leads them to design more narrow studies based on quantitative and behaviorist approaches to research.

There are few, if any, other structures beyond IRBs for researchers to review ethical dilemmas and implications of their own research. This narrow ethical review of research methods leaves researchers with little or no institutional support to reflect critically on the ethics of their research once it is underway. The typical location of IRBs outside of academic departments further reduces their effectiveness. Though this independence may be meant to remove bias from the review process, it also leads to uninformed and inappropriate review of discipline-specific research practices.

The problems with IRBs are magnified because there is seldom an appeal process through which students or their advisors can challenge IRB decisions and student progression in degree programs is dependent on timely IRB approval. As one student wrote in an email response to the IRB,

> I submitted my protocol before the required deadline, and repeatedly submitted revisions in a timely manner. However, this is my third set of revisions in four months. Due to this lengthy process and lack of approval, I have yet to register for my final required course, the Culminating Experience. I am concerned that any further delay in research approval will prevent me from graduating as planned in December, which would greatly inhibit my future career plans, as well as cost another semester of tuition. (personal communication, June 11, 2019)

Although the IRB held up the student's research, it was eventually accepted without major change and went on to win statewide research awards. Thus, this lengthy review, which nearly destroyed the student's chance to graduate, did not achieve any goals for protecting subjects.

"The directives and judgments of these boards have evolved," Marzano (2007) observed, "becoming considerably more restrictive, and they now represent a major bane and obstacle to the active researcher" (p. 424). When IRB review is seen primarily as an administrative hurdle, designed more to protect the university from litigation than to support ethical practices, it can lead to dismissal of the whole process by some professors, who may guide their students away from designing studies that fall under IRB purview. As one research advisor explained, "I'm just telling students now not to even bother, just to lie and say they are only doing a literature review. [IRB review] has gotten so bad" (personal communication, November 21, 2006). Or as a professor wrote in an email to an advisee:

> It is my current view that we can probably propose your study as a "curriculum development" project. . . . Framing the study in this way (at least for university approval purposes) would have one big advantage: it would allow us to avoid the onerous IRB nonsense. . . . [B]ecause it is framed in the context of curriculum and "normal educational practice," their view is that their obsessive scrutiny of human subjects involvement does not apply. . . . [T]his is a path that many, many students who are doing curriculum-related, applied work are taking. (personal communication, October 17, 2017)

The recognition among many professors and research advisors that IRBs offer only a rote and unreflective application of narrow and simplistic guidelines leads them to dismiss or ignore IRB guidelines. As a professor wrote in an email to an advisee, "Just give [the IRB committee] all the petty little stuff they want and you'll be home free. The good news is, your study will be approved once you've made these final silly minor changes. Then you/we can do anything you want with the study" (personal communication, December 23, 2013). In another example, a professor advised one of their undergraduates, "You just have to do this and then you can change everything later . . . just say what they want to hear" (personal communication, April 9, 2018). Thus, rather than helping researchers develop a process to carefully consider ethical decisions, IRBs may counterproductively lead to disengagement with ethical guidelines and reviews and minimal compliance with administrative directives. The flawed hegemony of IRBs shows both how institutional arrangements can lead students to design particular kinds of studies—those that are easier to pass through the IRB system—and how professors may collude with their students to obfuscate or hide data collection procedures. None of this leads to an enhanced level of ethical behavior.

To prepare researchers to act ethically involves developing their capacity to care for others, rather than giving them a checklist of requirements from an IRB: "If our objective is to produce people who will be prepared to care, we should concentrate on the development of empathy, not obedience to authority" (Noddings, 2010, p. 131). Instead of enforcing compliance with a list of approved ethical practices, research methodology courses could focus on cultivating an ethics of care. Empathy and care have long been feminized and devalued in the dominant discourse, yet they do not represent a "softer" approach: "Possibly no approach to ethics calls more urgently for critical thinking," argued Noddings (2010), "than care ethics":

> In care ethics, we put little faith in broad, abstract principles. . . . Nor do we substitute . . . a myriad of specific rules to replace universal principles . . . in every situation we must identify needs, analyze complex interactions, locate similarities and differences between present and past situations . . . consider the effects of our proposed current response on others in the web of care, and evaluate the resources at our disposal. (p. 132)

The ongoing analysis required to address ethical dilemmas requires far more resources than a brief online course, a single ethics lecture or chapter, and a one-time administrative IRB review, focused on form over content.

3.5 Research reporting conventions and constraints on research possibilities.

A particularly formulaic aspect of social science research is found in conventions for research reporting. Regardless of the type of research that social scientists conduct, they are expected to adhere to a five-part format from the scientific-empirical tradition: (a) purpose of study, (b) literature review, (c) methods, (d) results, and (e) discussion. Yet the normalized discourse of conventional research reporting is neither neutral nor inevitable:

> Beginning from the tentative hypotheses and moving to the research inquiry, the discovery of results, and the application of the findings for solving prior problems and confusions . . . reflects the heady mood of positivism in the early days of empirical science. The passive syntax and impersonal tone . . . maintain the pretense of objectivity, detachment, and neutrality, suppressing the agency of the researcher. The written product conveys the impression of infallible scholars mechanically driven along by their methodology and data to the inevitable findings. (Canagarajah, 1996, p. 323)

The conventional five-part research report leads to the maintenance of positivism in the field, privileges form over content, produces generic status quo findings, and constrains research possibilities.

Once researchers have stated their research purpose, they are expected to contextualize the intent, methods, and findings of their studies by developing a review of relevant prior research. The **literature review** is meant to assist readers in understanding the body of related available research and to inform them of the strengths and weaknesses of studies within that body. In contemporary practice in the physical and social sciences, there are three general types of literature review: narrative, systematic, and meta-analytic reviews. For some advisors, the accepted type of literature review is narrowed even further, limiting the review to empirical research studies from peer-reviewed journals published within the past 10 years.

Traditionally, **narrative reviews** are meant to critically appraise and summarize the literature relevant to an identified topic. Narrative reviews draw together major arguments in a field of discourse or provide a historical review of important aspects of related theory and practice. Since general guidelines for conducting narrative literature reviews may not always address the question of dealing with potentially large numbers of identified sources, these issues have been addressed in technocratic fashion in the social and physical sciences in recent decades by "systematic literature reviews" (SLRs). These reviews propose a strict scientistic protocol for the search and appraisal of literature. SLRs are claimed to introduce a "standardized method" for literature reviews that is replicable, transparent, objective, unbiased, and rigorous, and thus superior to other literature review approaches (Boell & Cecez-Kecmanovic, 2015).

Meta-analytic reviews, sometimes known as quantitative systematic reviews, apply an even more technocratic approach to measure the statistical effect size and impact of a number of studies relevant to a particular research question. A meta-analytic review has a systematic review as its first stage, followed by a statistical re-analysis of data with similar properties drawn from multiple studies that yield sufficient data (Rhoades, 2011). For example, a researcher may analyze every fifth article on a selected topic from a database to randomize their search, believing that it enhances validity. Yet claims that SLRs or meta-analyses provide superior quality are not justified, as they undermine critical scholarly engagement.

No matter which type of literature review is developed, all are steeped in epistemological beliefs and theoretical assumptions that constrain research. Literature reviews often reproduce the ideological assumptions of the prevailing paradigms of the era. Paradigms, as Kuhn (1969) asserted, are an unquestioned part of the landscape within which researchers operate. The given paradigm of any era sets limits on what questions might reasonably be asked and determines the scope of possible research.

After the literature review, most research reports require a section on methodology. The format of the section forces researchers to divorce the data collection process from the findings themselves. The result obscures both the research process and the data. In an attempt to rationalize and justify their research processes, many researchers may describe in a tidy fashion what was actually a messy research process. Students and researchers often retrospectively rewrite their Methodology sections to create the illusion that they followed a legitimate or "rigorous, linear, and scientific" process. A linear description of methods often belies the actual practices of doing research, and formulaic reports may mislead the reader to "believe that data were analyzed using the prescribed and familiar steps" (Tanggaard, 2013, p. 411). Conducting research is not a clear, linear process, where data collection proceeds data analysis and reporting; rather, the two may happen simultaneously, as St. Pierre wrote: "Data are collected during thinking, and for me, especially during writing" (as cited in Tanggaard, 2013, p. 416). Using passive voice with detached prose and divorcing methods from findings portray false coherence to the research process and offer no space for the researcher to address changes that may have occurred to their own perspectives during the research.

Research reports—like most scientific and informational texts—employ the third person (he, she, it, they) rather than the first person (I, we), without emotion, and they are most often written in the passive voice ("Multiple experimental interventions were implemented . . . "). This discursive format lends implied authority to a text by removing the identity of the narrator and by distancing controlled research events from everyday human experience. Following this discursive logic, in order to achieve a scientific tone, in academic historical texts "the events are chronologically recorded as they appear on the horizon of the story. No one speaks. The events seem to tell themselves" (White, 1990, p. 3). Novelists often employ the same device, yet their work is not seen as scientifically valid.

Researchers "prefer the passive voice, thinking that it makes writing more objective" (Booth et al., 2008, p. 263). They make passive voice statements such as "Eye movements were measured at tenth-of-second intervals" instead of active statements such as "We measured eye movements at tenth-of-second intervals." Both versions

> offer equally objective information, but their stories differ: one is about eye movements, the other about a person measuring them, who happens to also be the author. The first is supposed to be more 'objective' because it ignores the person and focuses on the movements. (Booth et al., 2008, p. 263)

Yet, simply avoiding "I" or "we" doesn't make writing more "objective," Booth et al. (2008) argued, "it simply changes the story" (p. 263). The researcher's story in most educational research reporting is obscured behind a veil of false objectivity. Though the first-person voice and close attention to detail in ethnographic writing may imply that researchers are photographically sharing the world as experienced firsthand, authors still make countless selections and decisions about what data to present and what to leave out.

The solution to detached, decontextualized research reporting practices cannot simply be to shift from a third-person objective tone to a first-person subjective inflection, or to move to active voice rather than passive voice. "Perfunctory 'I-dropping' is too weak a gesture to incorporate the splits and shifts in the subject position of the researcher" (Canagarajah, 1996, p. 325). Nor is it sufficient to add a brief statement on personal positionality, describing a presumably static social position ("I am a White, female, cisgender, middle-class professor"). Critical research, Canagarajah (1996) argued, requires "a more sustained and rigorous exploration of the ways the researcher's subjectivity influences the research process. Boxing this concern into a single section in a largely detached, univocally authored, realist text is unsatisfactory" (p. 325).

Some studies, especially those taking a feminist or postmodern approach, may insert the researcher's subjectivity, but even those works rarely explore how the research activity itself has impacted the authors' views or **positionality**: "The shifting/conflicting interests of the researcher—that is professional, personal, ideological—in carrying out the study are not acknowledged" (Canagarajah, 1996, p. 324).

Technocratic researchers are often discouraged from getting to know their subjects, beyond their essentialized identity characteristics, for fear that getting involved in the lives of subjects could bias the research findings. Even when researchers are in positions of power where they can take action to improve the lives of their subjects, they may feel that they must remain uninvolved to protect the integrity of their research. "Therefore, the rigorously self-examining attitude of the researcher and a caring personal investment in the life of the subjects demand new reporting conventions" (Canagarajah, 1996, p. 325).

Many researchers are profoundly affected by their fieldwork, yet complex self-reflection is generally "deemed irrelevant in the traditional report genre"

(Canagarajah, 1996, p. 324). Hidden in the conventions of tightly structured research reports are the "false starts, wrong moves, misleading tracks, and interpretative gambles that usually characterize the research process. There is a similar suppression of gaps, contradictions, and conflicts in the data for the sake of textual coherence" (Canagarajah, 1996, p. 324).

Most studies, instead of offering concrete details and stories, offer only broad, overly reduced findings in a dry and impersonal tone that is adopted to make the reports seem objective or scientific:

> Whilst appearing to promote the causes of accountability and transparency, the use of data can, in practice: conceal more than it reveals; invite misinterpretation; and worst of all, have a perverse effect on the behavior of professionals. . . . All this suggests that great care needs to be exercised in deciding what evidence is collected and, indeed, how it is used. (Ainscow, 2005, pp. 119, 120)

In the traditional Findings section of the research report, subjects exist only in and through the voice of the researcher. In conventional reports, there is

> little room for 'authentic' representation of the informant's views as the researcher eventually holds the pen. It is the researcher who enjoys the authority to choose and organize the words of the informants, apart from providing coherence for the text with an overarching generalization or theory (that would neutralize any tensions). (Canagarajah, 1996, p. 326)

Many academics and graduate students rely on external funding for their research, and these agencies "often predefine problem frames to fit their agendas" (Nespor & Groenke, 2014, p. 1005). In many cases, researchers are funded by foundations or corporations to generate findings to support a particular program or policy. Researchers in this situation may be required to channel data and skew findings to match their funders' perspectives. "Data are never presented in 'full,'" observed Fine (1993), "and choices are inevitable" (p. 287). One of Fine's colleagues, for instance, reported withholding data in a study that might have harmed perception of the ethnic group he studied, saying that the members of the group already had "enough trouble."

In one research project funded by a foundation that promoted college access for first-generation students, researchers conducted and analyzed hundreds of interviews and generated more than 30 findings. When sharing a draft with the funder, the lead researcher was told to "boil them down to a half dozen or so" and "line them up" more closely with the foundation's stated policy agenda (personal communication, December 5, 2018). Upon reviewing the draft findings again, the funder restated again that the report was too long, asking for a shortened document that offered clearer, simpler policy recommendations even more in line with the foundation's priorities. The research team finally submitted a severely truncated final document that did little to reflect the complex findings originally generated. Soon after the submission, there was a major staff shift at the foundation, and the report was never disseminated. More than a year of intense research work, funded at close to $300,000, was left on the shelf because it was no longer of interest to the new leadership. The politics of funding agencies can shape which research findings are reported—or whether they are even reported at all.

Although researchers may seek to generate findings that challenge existing paradigms, doing so is rare because of normalizing pressures that generally lead to the persistent reporting of status quo findings on predetermined topics. "The academic field makes certain kinds of problem frames seem more viable as academic currency than others" (Nespor & Groneke, 2014, p. 1005). The top-down nature of how research is funded, as well as how graduate education is conducted, encourages "regurgitative mastery": "The micropolitics of programs pressure students to attach themselves to established faculty members and align their work with the problems that interest the single professor whose decisions determine their immediate futures" (Nespor & Groeneke, 2014, p. 1005).

In an effort to make findings generalizable, many research reports exclude specific details, providing only reductive summaries with little utility for practice. An instance of this can be found in the assessment activities of a countywide nonprofit in California, which made a large investment in a third-party evaluation firm to monitor its philanthropic initiatives. The firm chose a standardized assessment called the Kindergarten Observation Form, which required all kindergarten teachers to have a substitute teacher for the day while they administered a one-to-one assessment with each student. The teachers experienced frustration not only because of the missed class time but also because most of the data collected in this assessment had already been collected in other school assessments, amounting to needless duplication.

The findings in the evaluators report were limited to the following generic statements:

- Children who were well fed and rested were significantly more prepared for school.
- Children who were engaged in family activities by their parents were better prepared for school.
- Children who worked on their skills prior to school were more ready for kindergarten.
- Children who were involved in various activities were ready for school. (Applied Survey Research, 2012, p. 19)

The findings contributed no new knowledge, and as one kindergarten teacher said, "That wasn't surprising to us." This kind of reductionism fails to provide educators with practical findings that address the problems they face. "To avoid the often boring and superficial character of such descriptions," Tanggaard (2013) argued for "the insertion of more flesh and blood in research reports, using the words of everyday actors, re-working and engaging in dialogue with them" (p. 416).

The widespread acceptance of a technocratic research approach often fails to offer actionable findings for educators. Changing this would require reinvestment in teachers themselves, funding professional development time for them to reflect on their practice and to access the research of their colleagues. Local ongoing inquiry can help educators develop research practices that provide relevant action possibilities, rather than top-down, generic prescriptions.

Although the conventions for research reporting are severely limited, they do not need to be entirely rejected. They can be reimagined to open up third spaces for critical engagement. Given the limitations of existing approaches to literature reviews, one alternative direction is a hermeneutic approach. As a theory of interpretation that deals with questions of meaning of texts, **hermeneutics** provides a theoretical foundation for understanding and interpreting findings and the research reporting process. Gadamer (1976) approached understanding as a practical engagement through dialogue between readers and texts. For Gadamer, understanding texts—including auditory, visual, and written texts—is always a translation in a concrete sociohistorical and cultural context. There is no correct or universal interpretation of a text outside of history, culture, or standpoint.

A hermeneutic approach to research analysis and reporting involves developing an understanding that is iterative in nature. It encompasses literature searching, data collection, classifying and mapping, critical assessment, and argument development—all accompanied by continuing reinterpretation. The hermeneutic approach emphasizes continuous engagement with and gradual development of a text during which increased understanding and insights are developed. According to hermeneutics, understanding is not a linear process but a spiraling one that is informed by successive understandings. The hermeneutic framework therefore provides a theoretical foundation for the view of research reporting as a practical system that is constantly changing (Boell & Cecez-Kecmanovic, 2014).

Another alternative approach to research writing is **critical discourse analysis** (CDA). From the perspective of CDA, research publications are communicative processes that occur in a social setting and thus reflect social structures, norms, and discourses. Influenced by Foucault (1972, 1980), discourse is viewed as the history of knowledge and practice, and as the process by which knowledge and practice become codified and normalized. CDA examines the historical roots of beliefs and practices and the structures and powerful actors that influence the adoption and continuation of beliefs and practices. Power is a crucial element of this perspective because power imbalances lead to hegemonic ideas and structures. Critically informed research reporting can provide the means to assess assumptions and search for broader research perspectives (Wall et al., 2015).

Standard research methods instruction narrows and idealizes the research process and eliminates critical analysis with its taken-for-granted scientistic superiority. As a result, professors and research advisors spend more time on form than content and rarely accept anything other than research studies that adhere to the narrow methodological norms, or even more narrowly to their own pet approach. At every stage of the research process, technocratic methods constrain research possibilities and normalize false binaries that diminish the perceived legitimacy of other paradigms. Students' interests and inquiries grounded from their own experience are generally dismissed as "unresearchable." Their research questions are recast in scientistic terms that force them to generate simplistic relationships among reductive variables. To enhance the validity and reliability of their studies, students are further encouraged to use already validated instruments instead of producing their own forms of inquiry. This consigns students to normalized, hegemonic research constructs. Standard conventions for study design and research reporting further force students to describe their work in linear terms that obfuscate the messy, episodic practices of collecting and analyzing data. The emphasis on form over content throughout the research process not only narrows research possibilities but also leads to the production of generic findings that are seldom useful to educators in practice.

References

Ainscow, M. (2005). Developing inclusive education systems: What are the levers for change? *Journal of Educational Change, 6*(2), 109–124.

Allwood, C. M. (2012). The distinction between qualitative and quantitative research methods is problematic. *Qual Quant, 46*(5), 1417–1429.

Apel, K. O. (1984). *Understanding and explanation: A transcendental and pragmatic perspective.* MIT Press.

Applied Survey Research. (2012). *School readiness in Marin County: School report: Venetia Valley Elementary School.* San Rafael School District.

Barad, K. (2007). *Meeting the universe halfway: Quantum physics and the entanglement of matter and meaning.* Duke University Press.

Beneventi, A. (2016). The Annemarie Roeper method of qualitative assessment: My journey. *Roeper Review, 38*(4), 252–257.

Blakely, E. (2007). *Interrupted narratives: Cultural invisibility in the classroom* [Unpublished master's thesis]. San Francisco State University.

Boell, S. K., & Cecez-Kecmanovic, D. (2015). On being 'systematic' in literature reviews in IS. *Journal of Information Technology, 30*, 161–173.

Booth, W. C., Colomb, G. C., & Williams, J. M. (2008). *The craft of research* (3rd ed.). The University of Chicago Press.

Bosk, C. L., & De Vries, R. G. (2004). Bureaucracies of mass deception: Institutional Review Boards and the ethics of ethnographic research. *The ANNALS of the American Academy of Political and Social Science, 595*, 249–263.

Brinkmann, S. (2013). *John Dewey: Science for a changing world.* Transaction Publishers.

Canagarajah, A. S. (1996). From critical research practice to critical research reporting. *TESOL Quarterly, 30*(2), 321–331.

Carlson, J. F., Geisinger, K. F., & Jonson, J. L. (Eds.). (2020). *The twenty-first mental measurements yearbook.* Buros Center for Testing.

Clifford, J. (1988). *The predicament of culture: Twentieth-century ethnography, literature, and art.* Harvard University Press.

Cohen, L., Manion, L., & Morrison, K. (2011). *Research methods in education* (7th ed.). Routledge.

Crenshaw, K. (1991). Mapping the margins: Intersectionality, identity politics, and violence against women of color. *Stanford Law Review, 43*(6), 1241–1299.

Creswell, J. W. (2012). *Educational research: Planning, conducting, and evaluating quantitative and qualitative research.* Pearson.

Dear, P. (1991). *The literary structure of scientific argument: Historical studies.* University of Pennsylvania Press.

Deuchar, R. (2015). Dilemmas, deception and ethical decision-making: Insights from a transatlantic ethnographer. In K. Bhopal & R. Deuchar (Eds.), *Researching marginalized groups* (pp. 62–74). Routledge.

Dewey, J. (1891). Moral theory and practice. *International Journal of Ethics, 1*, 186–203.

Dewey, J. (1896). The reflex arc concept in psychology. *The Psychological Review, 3*(4), 357–370.

Dewey, J. (1916). *Democracy and education.* The Free Press.

Erickson, F., & Gutierrez, K. (2002). Comment: Culture, rigor, and science in educational research. *Educational Researcher, 31*(8), 21–24.

Fine, G. A. (1993). Ten lies of ethnography: Moral dilemmas of field research. *Journal of Contemporary Ethnography, 22*(3), 267–294.

Foucault, M. (1972). *The archaeology of knowledge and the discourse on language.* Pantheon Books.

Foucault, M. (1980). *Power/Knowledge: Selected interviews and other writings, 1972–77* (C. Gordon, Ed.). Pantheon Books.

Fraenkel, J., Wallen, N., & Hyun, H. (2012). *How to design and evaluate research in education.* McGraw Hill Education.

Gadamer, H. G. (1976). *Philosophical hermeneutics.* University of California Press.

Habermas, J. (1971). *Knowledge and human interests.* Beacon Press.

Holzkamp, K. (2013). *Psychology from the standpoint of the subject: Selected writings of Klaus Holzkamp.* Palgrave MacMillan.

Juelskjær, M. (2013). Gendered subjectivities of spacetimematter. *Gender and Education, 25*(6), 754–768.

Juelskjær, M., & Schwennesen, N. (2012). Intra-active entanglements: An interview with Karen Barad. *Kvinder, Kon, & Forkskning, 1–2*, 10–24.

Katzew, I. (1996). Casta painting: Identity and social stratification in colonial Mexico. In *New world orders: Casta painting and colonial Latin America.* Americas Society Art Gallery.

Kuhn, T. S. (1969) *The structure of scientific revolutions.* University of Chicago Press.

Lakoff, G., & Johnson, M. (1980). *Metaphors we live by.* University of Chicago Press.

Lane, E.S. & Harris, S.E. (2015). A new tool for measuring student behavioral engagement in large university classes. *Research and Teaching, 44*(6), 83–91.

Lave, J. (2019). *Learning and everyday life: Access, participation, and changing practice.* Cambridge University Press.

Lenz Taguchi, H. (2010). *Going beyond the theory/practice divide in early childhood education: Introducing an intra-active pedagogy.* Routledge.

Lincoln, Y. S., & Guba, E. G. (1985). *Naturalistic inquiry*. Sage.

Marx, K. (1971). *Capital: Vol. I. A critical analysis of capitalist production*. Progress Publishers. (Original work published 1887)

Marzano, M. (2007). Informed consent, deception, and research freedom in qualitative research: A cross-cultural comparison. *Qualitative Inquiry, 13*(3), 417–436.

Nespor, J., & Groenke, S. L. (2014). Ethics, problem framing, and training in qualitative inquiry. *Qualitative Inquiry, 15*(6), 996–1012.

Nielsen, K. (1999). *Musical apprenticeship: Learning at the Academy of Music as socially situated.* Psychology Institute, Aarhus University.

Noddings, N. (2010). *The maternal factor: Two paths to morality*. University of California Press.

Ollman, B. (1976). *Alienation: Marx's conception of man in capitalist society* (Vol. 9). Cambridge University Press.

Piaget, J. (1951). *The psychology of intelligence*. Routledge.

Pollock, M. (2005). Race bending: 'Mixed' youth practicing strategic racialization in California. In S. Maria & E. Soep (Eds.), *Youthscapes: The popular, the national, and the global* (pp. 43–63). University of Pennsylvania Press.

Rhoades, E. A. (2011). Literature reviews. *The Volta Review, 111*(3), 353368.

Saldaña, J. (2015). *The coding manual for qualitative researchers*. Sage.

Tanggaard, L. (2013). Troubling methods in qualitative inquiry and beyond. *Europe's Journal of Psychology, 9*(3), 409–418.

Thompson, I., & Mackiewicz, J. (2014). Questioning in writing center conferences. *The Writing Center Journal, 33*(2), 37–70.

Tuhiwai Smith, L. (1999). *Decolonizing methodologies: Research and indigenous peoples*. Zed Books.

U.S. Department of Education. (2018). *Companion guidelines on replication and reproducibility in education research: A supplement to the Common Guidelines for Education Research and Development*. Institute of Education Services. https://ies.ed.gov/pdf/CompanionGuidelinesReplicationReproducibility.pdf

Vidich, A. J., & Lyman, S. M. (1998). Qualitative methods: Their history in sociology and anthropology. In N. Denzin & Y. S. Lincoln (Eds.), *The landscape of qualitative research* (pp. 23–44). Sage.

Wall, J. D., Stahl, B. C., & Salam, A. F. (2015). Critical discourse analysis as a review methodology: An empirical example. *Communications of the Association for Information Systems, 34*(11), 257–285.

Weber, M. (2011). *Methodology of social sciences*. Routledge.

White, H. (1990). *The content of the form: Narrative discourse and historical representation*. Johns Hopkins University Press.

FOUR

Reconceptualizing Learning in Educational Research

EDUCATIONAL RESEARCH IS NARROWLY PREDICATED on the modernist notion that the individual is primary, which ignores how social relations are entangled in learning and reduces it to the internal mental process of acquiring knowledge or skills. Educational research further equates learning with teaching and sees it as its direct product. This has limited the scope and depth of educational research practice, turning it into little more than the testing of commodified best practices. As decades of standardized testing results confirm, technocratic measures of learning are at best predictive only of students' family income and education level. It is useless, therefore, to reduce learning to a simplistic measurable outcome. If educational researchers are going to move past the limits of technocratic research, they need a reconceptualization of learning that is not focused on individual outcomes of isolated teaching techniques but rather on learners' changing participation in practice. Taking a dialectical view of learning—one that does not separate learners from their social relations, the content, or the context of their learning—requires expanding third spaces for inquiry.

The widely accepted standard definition of learning is not neutral; it is part of the neoliberal discourse of commodification, which turns schools into producers and students into consumers of knowledge products. The continuing demand for precise measurement of knowledge products has led to the predominance of student learning outcomes (SLOs) and program learning outcomes (PLOs) in education, where "the process of learning is grasped as an isolated subject's secluded and parceled acquisition of a pre-given and secluded object of knowledge" (Dreier, 2008, pp. 88, 93). This functionalist definition abstracts learning, ignoring the complexity of social relations and the material conditions of learning contexts.

4.1 Problems with specifying learning outcomes and the myth of transfer.

Educators commonly perceive students as empty vessels, waiting to be filled. Teachers' expected role is to deposit information and then withdraw it in the form of performance tests. In this metaphor, the products of learning are imagined as distinct units, property, or possessions, and most schools are based on this commodification of learning. Freire (1970) referred to this as a "banking style" of education:

> Instead of communicating, the teacher issues communiqués and makes deposits which the students patiently receive. . . . Knowledge is a gift bestowed by those who consider themselves knowledgeable upon those whom they consider to know nothing. . . . The more students work at storing the deposits entrusted to them, the less they develop the critical consciousness which would result from their intervention in the world as transformers of that world. (pp. 58, 60)

The banking style of education not only makes learners passive recipients of knowledge products but also reinforces representationalism, specifically the idea that there is a clear distinction between the individual learner and an objective body of knowledge.

Educators further assume that learning is the direct product of teaching. This assumption most often takes the form of curricula as measures of input and student grades as measures of outcome.

> In school's official, institutionally fixed understanding, learning is normally regarded as a direct result of teaching, and since teaching is viewed as something that can be planned administratively, the learning processes of pupils automatically appear to be plannable as well. (Holzkamp, 2013, p. 118)

Following this assumption, educational institutions fixate on the administrative planning of learning to provide students with uniform delivery of curriculum products. Presuming that learning is administratively plannable, educators spend a great deal of time and effort developing ways to articulate desired SLOs or PLOs and ways of measuring them.

SLOs and PLOs are discussed endlessly in staff meetings, professional development sessions, and parent–teacher conferences. Lists of SLOs and

PLOs that reflect approved governmental or institutional standards appear on course syllabi, curriculum packages, school websites, grant proposals, and report cards. Teacher preparation is frequently focused on how to create lessons that specify and produce these anticipated outcomes. Much professional development time is spent on articulating expected SLOs and PLOs of educational activities at student and program levels. Leaders at one institution, for example, elaborated a process for identifying and assessing learning outcomes; they referred to this process as the "full SLO cycle":

1. Write or revise SLOs and identify the measures for assessing their attainment for each course, state-approved certificate and degree, and student services program. Incorporate SLOs in course-of-record outlines, course syllabi, and the college catalog.
2. Map course SLOs to the department's program SLOs (PSLOs) and to the institutional SLOs (ISLOs). In case of revision, ensure that SLOs are still correctly mapped.
3. Implement SLOs in courses and instructional and student support programs and introduce them to students early in the semester.
4. Collect and report data on student achievement of the SLOs.
5. Review the results on student attainment of the course [SLOs, PSLOs, and ISLOs].
6. Develop and implement a Course Improvement Plan . . . to improve student learning and achievement.
7. Use the program review process to assess student achievement of each of the [PSLOs] and on the basis of those results to develop Program Improvement Plans.
8. Use the results on student achievement of the ISLOs to develop an institutional improvement plan to increase the progress students make toward acquiring the competencies associated with each of the [ISLOs]. (Santa Barbara City College [SBCC], 2018)

In the full SLO cycle, only the third step of a total of eight ("Implement SLOs in courses . . . ") alludes to actual instruction or interaction with students; the other seven steps specify administrative planning and measurement procedures.

Learning outcomes developed in SLO cycles are carefully examined for their fidelity to mandated curriculum standards, evaluated directly at the local level by administrators, coaches, and peers in professional development groups and indirectly at the national level through standardized testing. Throughout the process, educators are expected to accept unquestioningly that learning is a direct product of teaching that can be readily measured. Emphasis on measuring observable learning outcomes is a key component of the influential standards-based education movement that has spread rapidly beginning in the 1980s and 1990s in the United States, United Kingdom, and many other countries in K-12 and higher education systems. Spurred by governmental mandates of full compliance, educators uncritically produce and reproduce tautological and overlapping PLOs and SLOs. This process characterizes professional development at all educational levels, amounting to an unthinking and enforced administrative compliance on the part of educators.

Most departments are required to produce SLOs or PLOs for all scheduled learning activities, ranging from short workshops to course-level, department-level, and institutional outcomes. For example, the following SLOs are stated for a two-hour undergraduate workshop called Essentials of Research offered by a campus tutorial center:

> After attending this workshop, students should be able to do the following:
>
> 1. Create a writing plan for a research paper.
> 2. Access research resources online and at the library.
> 3. Understand the concepts of source evaluation. (SBCC, 2019)

Such SLOs are readily approved by administrators even though it is unlikely that students could achieve such comprehensive outcomes after only two hours of instruction. SLO data are presented on the college's website in pie charts that claim to demonstrate the tutorial center's effectiveness for each workshop (SBCC, 2019). Such SLO data often have little to do with concern for student progress and are used primarily as justification for program continuance. Administrators make policy decisions based on such data with no scrutiny of the criteria for how an SLO, such as "Understand the concepts of source evaluation," is generated.

Recognizing the difficulty of measuring learning outcomes, one university's guide to writing PLOs stated the following:

> Measurable PLOs: PLOs should be written in such a way that it is easy to imagine a project, report, exam, quiz, survey, or other piece of student work that could be use[d] to assess how well a student has learned the PLO. This is typically achievable by using active verbs to describe the PLO, such as explain, analyze, or design, rather than passive verbs such as appreciate, become familiar with, or understand. (CSU Fullerton, 2019)

The suggestion that "understanding" is not a desired outcome of learning because it cannot be readily measured may appear rational to educators in the contemporary policy climate (Gadamer, 1976). This view, however, reflects a limited positivist construction of education. A focus on only those outcomes that can be observed and measured narrows educational processes and mischaracterizes complexities of learning.

Even when active verbs are used or SLOs are stated as simply as "will count to 10 without errors," these measures fail to account for how students approach or experience the task, or whether they perform the counting task easily or haltingly. The measures also fail to relate whether the student counts with understanding or not. Although the specification of measurable learning outcomes gives the impression of precision and accountability, learning outcomes are difficult to measure. "The illusion of measured learning," wrote Lave and McDermott (2002), "makes substantial what is not and reifies it into numbers" (p. 21). Concrete criteria for measuring academic success via SLOs are therefore an illusion. Their clarity, explicitness, and objectivity are spurious, argued Hussey and Smith (2002). No matter how minutely learning activities are articulated, objectified, and measured, Holzkamp (2013) suggested, they rarely map onto the student experience of learning. As Lenz Taguchi (2010) wrote,

> Pedagogy can never be about planning exactly what kinds of learning processes will take place, or what kinds of learning will be achieved. There is no way to predict exact learning outcomes . . . which is why teaching and learning needs to be thought about in other ways. (p. 60)

Dominant approaches to measuring learning further assume that an individual's skill acquisition is stable, cumulative, transferable, and possible to measure in a single, one-time assessment. Yet, as Colaizzi (1978) described, the process of learning something cannot be reduced to one-time performance measures:

> For all of us there are certain life lessons which we read or hear spoken hundreds of times before they finally click in. Until they do click in, we haven't really learned them, regardless of how glibly we can verbalize them. Prior to the point where they become significantly interwoven in our existence, they are merely bits of information that we have acquired. (p. 127)

Schooling depends on the assumption that transfer of learning readily occurs as students seamlessly apply school-learned knowledge to new situations. Accordingly, teachers are trained to emphasize global skills, believing that the way to strengthen learning transfer is to focus on abstract knowledge applicable in several different contexts. From a technocratic perspective, "knowledge is central, not the person or social interaction, and it is knowledge that is moved [unchanged] from one task in one context to another" (Nielsen, 2009, p. 61). Yet Scribner and Cole (1981) and Lave (1988) suggest that learning does not transfer from one context to another as educators expect; it is dependent on specific social contexts. They question the decontextualization of knowledge in schooling. Lack of performance of a particular skill cannot be generalized, these theorists claim, either to an expectation of nonperformance on other tasks or to the absence of the necessary underlying abilities.

What may appear to educators to be underlying, transferable, basic or global skills (such as grammar structures or math operations) often do not appear that way to learners. Learners may more readily focus on the surface content rather than the presumed underlying skills. For example, when teachers give students sample essays on volcanoes and drug use to review how the authors use topic sentences, they assume that the surface content is immaterial. Yet students may not see it that way, and they may be drawn into the context of the topics instead of the teacher's expected learning outcomes—identifying topic sentences. Scribner and Cole (1981), Lave (1988), and Rogoff (2003) all argue that most forms of problem-solving, reasoning, and computing are heavily reliant on the context of their use and should not be considered or taught apart from situated contexts. Nielsen (2009), too, suggested that

> learning is not merely a matter of understanding something specific in one context (such as learning the skills needed to solve a specific kind of problem); it is also a matter of learning about the contexts in which to apply this kind of activity (e.g., learning where and in relation to whom and which kind of activities it is relevant to apply the skills to solve a specific kind of problem). (pp. 67–68)

While teachers may expect students to acquire global skills that they can transfer, students may instead be focused primarily on performing behaviors expected by teachers. Students complying with particular teacher demands to produce SLOs, then, may be doing what Holzkamp (2013) called *defensive learning*. Defensive learning describes all the activities and gestures involved in "doing school," such as sitting still at a desk, raising a hand, and looking at the assigned page or the instructor. These behaviors are deployed defensively by students as evidence of learning, often measured as time on task or engagement. What students actually learn in schools, then, may have less to do with the content teachers think they are providing and more with "how to be" in school. As Lave and Wenger (1991) argued, "Learning how to 'do' school appropriately may be a major part of what school teaches" (p. 107).

The constant need for teachers to regulate student attention and behavior contributes to what Holzkamp (2013) called *satisficing*—performances such as sitting still or raising hands, which demonstrate that students understand what teachers wish them to do and not what the students have learned. Since teachers are required to ensure that students have equal access to the curriculum and to spend required time on task, they are often compelled to discipline as marginal or disruptive those student interactions that take them away from producing specified SLOs. Artifacts of technocratic rigidity are present in nearly every classroom, from behavior management systems that track and label students' "readiness to learn," to class points or "brain bucks" that reward time on task or other actions related to student engagement. The current competitive school ranking system relies on the physical presence of students (holding parents criminally responsible if their children are chronically absent or absent for unexcused reasons) and on their mental presence (holding students responsible for attention to tasks and punishing disruptions). Defining achievement in terms of observed individual gain, Nielsen (2016) also argued, "naturalizes the idea that social-struggle as competition between individuals is the structuring force in the development of society" (p. 141).

In prioritizing the production of SLOs, schools have become what Foucault (1977) called sites of uninterrupted examination, making perpetual comparisons a repeated ritual of power. Examinations enable teachers, while transmitting their knowledge, to transform the students into an entire field of knowledge. The examination situates individuals in an entire range of documents that encapsulate them, making it possible to capture and fix them. The technique of examination makes each individual into a "case." This case can then be described, judged, measured, compared to others; through this classification students are objectified, and pedagogy, in turn, operates as a science (Foucault, 1977). The pressure placed on students to produce SLOs that conform to school standards can dehumanize and alienate students, socializing them to "forget their own existence" (Colaizzi, 1978). To challenge these problems requires a reconceptualization of learning, with a shift away from technocratic measurement and evaluation practices.

4.2 Learning as legitimate peripheral participation.

The focus in education on accountability structures and the precise measurement of SLOs can result in ignoring social relations. Learning is not, Firth and Wagner (1997) argued, "an individual phenomenon . . . of private thoughts . . . transferred from brain to brain, but a social and negotiable product of interaction" (p. 290). To neglect social relations is thus to neglect learning, yet that is often what educational researchers do. The idea that learning is a social process is not new, but it continues to be poorly understood and only intermittently applied in the field of education.

Vygotsky (1981) first argued in the early 20th century that learning is a social function of communities rather than individuals. His sociocultural approach to learning was not introduced in the West until the 1980s because of the barriers placed by the Cold War. Vygotsky claimed that a child develops concepts and skills first in interactions with others (on the "intermental" plane) and later internalizes these new mental functions (on the "intramental" plane), transforming them in the process: "Even when we turn to mental processes, their nature remains quasi-social. In their own private sphere, human beings retain the functions of social interaction" (Vygotsky, 1981, p. 164). To illustrate, Vygotsky showed how remembering, which is usually presumed to be an individual mental function, is often a social process, as when a teacher or parent asks a child a series of questions about the location of a missing object.

Dewey (1922) argued similarly that learning is not an individual's acquisition of information about how the world "out there" is, but a social process of developing a complex, flexible set of "pre-dispositions for action." Even an apparently internal process such as thinking, Dewey believed, is interdependent and constantly connected to material contexts, social habits, and activity. He defined thinking as "dramatic rehearsal (in imagination) of various competing possible lines of action" (Dewey, 1922, p. 132). This combination of reflection and action, he argued, leads to knowledge: "Knowing is itself an activity, 'it is literally something which we do'" (Dewey, as cited in Biesta & Burbules, 2003, p. 46). Dewey (1910) warned against giving precedence to abstract knowledge or general principles: "When this . . . occurs, principles become fossilized and rigid; they lose their inherent vitality, their self-impelling power" (p. 213). He maintained that no general principle is a self-contained thing, separable and independent from specific use in practice.

Lave and Wenger (1991), too, argued that learning is not something that happens within individual minds but is "a contextual occurrence," something that happens between participants as a distributed part of social practice (Christensen, 2016, p. 126). **Situated learning**, as Lave and Wenger described it, is not a direct product of teaching, nor does it occur exclusively or more effectively in formal settings such as classrooms. Learning, they claimed, occurs as a part of everyday life in numerous contexts. Context cannot be removed, as Gee (2001) stated:

> The meaning of words, phrases, and sentences are always "situated," that is "customized" to the actual contexts we are in. Here "context" means not just the words, deeds, and things that surround our words or deeds, but also our purposes, values, and intended courses of action and interaction. (p. 138)

What counts as grammatically correct, for example, always depends on context. As Gee described, it might be formally correct for someone to say, "Pardon me, but could you please tell me if you have a match?" but it would be wrong to say this in a bar, where "Gotta match?" would be more appropriate.

Lave and Wenger (1991) redefined learning as changing participation in what they term **communities of practice**. "A community of practice is a socially arranged space where language and meaning are created and maintained" (Nielsen, 1999, p. 23). Any social group can potentially be a community of practice, from sports teams to musical groups, book clubs, gangs, and management teams. What distinguishes a community of practice from the general understanding of a community is that the group has an identity connected to a shared domain of interest. Its members engage in joint activities, share information, and care about their relationships or standing among others in the group. Participants in any community of practice are all involved, to varying degrees, in carrying out the activities related to a mutual product or common task (Christensen, 2016). They have a shared repertoire of tools, stories, gestures, concepts, and other artifacts.

Communities of practice are not always acknowledged as formal groups. For example, teachers who meet daily in the lunchroom may become a community of practice, even if they do not always recognize how their interactions function as a source of knowledge for dealing with students, administrators, pedagogy, and the demands of their jobs. Other terms that scholars have used to describe communities of practice include "landscapes of participation" and "fields of activity" (Nielsen & Kvale, 2006). In these landscapes, fields, or communities of practice, meaning is a process, always negotiated, never complete, "carrying historical continuity as well as change" (p. 123). The participants in a community of practice provide "the interpretative support necessary for making sense of its heritage. . . . The social structure of this practice, its power relations, and its conditions for legitimacy define possibilities for learning (i.e., for legitimate peripheral participation)" (Lave & Wenger, 1991, p. 98).

Lave and Wenger (1991) used the term **legitimate peripheral participation** to describe how learning takes place as new members of a community of practice become increasingly knowledgeable and integrated into the social group. They investigated, for example, the ways in which newcomers to Alcoholics Anonymous meetings were gradually included in the group. Through listening to the stories and discussions of long-term members, newcomers to Alcoholics Anonymous meetings gradually adopted the discourse of the group. It was expected that it would take time before they were fully participating members; the newcomers occupied a legitimate position on the periphery. With ongoing modeling, shared stories, and support of the group, newcomers began to take on the group's discourse, participate more fully, and eventually many learned to cope with their addiction and become recovered alcoholics.

Lave and Wenger (1991) argued that when it comes to learning "the issue of conferring legitimacy is more important than the issue of providing teaching" (p. 92). Yet legitimate peripheral participation is not meant to be prescriptive for teacher practice. Lave (2011) claimed that it does not suggest an alternative or inherently better form of instruction, but it does suggest a shift in approach to research on learning.

Instead of discussions and planning of SLOs, researchers could begin to examine who students are becoming within changing contexts of communities of practice. Reconceptualizing learning as legitimate peripheral participation opens up the kinds of questions that educational researchers can ask. Instead of inquiring about the most effective techniques for teaching a particular skill or how to achieve a designated learning outcome, research could focus instead on the historical constitution of everyday practices and how subjects constitute themselves through their participation in those practices (Lave, 2019). This kind of ethnographic research does not demand reliability; it accepts that communities are not fixed or stable.

If educators dissolve the binary that erroneously makes the social and external world separate or opposite from the individual or personal, then they can recognize how "the human subject is considered as formed in and through the community of practice" (Christensen, 2016, p. 132). The individual cannot be isolated from context; thus, "the-subject-in-the-world" should be the smallest unit of analysis in educational research. It makes little sense to compare individual proficiency to baseline data or to measure skills isolated from context, as currently practiced.

Adopting a situated perspective on learning in educational research implies investigating learners' perspectives on their participation in communities of practice—their reasons for acting across contexts and how this relates to their own self-understanding and recognition by others: "When conducting empirical research, this means that trajectories of change and the ways in which we shape/are shaped into the persons we are and become through (more or less) participation in changing social practices over time are pivotal" (Rasmussen, 2016, p. 233). This entails asking the following kinds of research questions: What kinds of participation are supported, limited, or discouraged inside and outside the classroom—how and why? How do distinct material, institutional, and social arrangements support or contradict each other and how do they expand or contract students' participation? How are understandings of appropriate or normative participation generated and how do they impact students' possible lines of action?

4.3 Learning as identity formation.

Participation in any community of practice confers a sense of belonging and involves shaping an identity. As Lave and Wenger (1991) suggested,

> Moving toward full participation in practice involves not just a greater commitment of time, intensified effort, more and broader responsibilities within the community, and more difficult and risky tasks, but more significantly an increasing sense of identity as a master practitioner. (p. 111)

Through participation in various communities of practice, learners gradually become artists, chemists, dancers, English speakers, programmers, readers, chefs, writers, and so on. Learning involves gaining access to everything that membership entails; it involves *becoming*: "To be a participant in a community of practice is thus the starting point in an understanding of ourselves and the world" (Nielsen, 2016, p. 153). Plauborg (2018) concurred that knowledge acquisition cannot be separated from identity development: "Our continuous becoming is entangled in our knowledge acquisition and vice versa." Talking about students' identities and their processes of becoming cannot remain on the sidelines of educational discourse.

Identity development does not happen in an isolated or linear way, where an essentialized, adult, autonomous self slowly emerges. Hall (1996) argued that identity is a process of articulation that involves the marking of symbolic boundaries. It is neither an essential, internal state nor the exclusive result of external factors but instead a hybrid, ongoing process that involves discursive work, material arrangements and the norms and social stock of knowledge that students navigate at school, at home, in the community, and the larger marketplace.

Growing up involves a "hybridization pastiche process of stitching together an identity like trying on clothes, becoming your own hybrid, blending, shaping, and putting together something that's a range of cultures" (Luke, as cited in Besley, 2003, p. 170). Identity-making, especially for youth in a globalized era, "is about being between 16 or 18 different worlds. . . . It's about navigating a sea of texts. Each one of these texts is trying to position you, sell you, define you" (Luke, as cited in Besley, 2003, p. 170). Identity, likewise, cannot be described by singular labels of nation-state, ethnicity, or language.

Commonly used labels in educational research (Latinx, White, African American, immigrant, English Language Learner) fail to account for the hybrid, overlapping identities students may take on: "Even when young people are not themselves traveling across national borders, or leaving their own bedrooms, they can find themselves, implicated within transnational networks" (Maira & Soep, 2005, p. xix). Hybridity, or "how cultural forms and practices intermingle and traverse social boundaries," challenges the reductive, homogenous cultural and linguistic identities assigned by schools (Lam, 2006, p. 217; also see Bhabha, 1994; Clifford, 1988). There is a need, wrote Appadurai (1996), to reconceptualize the "landscape of group identity" to reflect current transnational conditions in which "groups are no longer tightly territorialized, spatially bounded, historically unselfconscious, or culturally homogenous" (p. 191).

Despite 21st-century rhetoric to prepare students for global citizenship, most schools continue to construct and maintain hierarchies that privilege English and other colonial languages and discourage code-switching, mixing, or blending of languages. "Words distorted by English," wrote Anzaldúa (1999), "are known as anglicisms or *pochismos*" (p. 78). Spanish anglicisms, such as *bola* for ball, *carpeta* for carpet, *watchar* for watch, or *parkiar* for park, are not incorrect but are instead products of cultural evolution that reflects speakers' identities. Eradicating students' multilingual discourse from the classroom becomes an exclusionary act, alienating students from academics: "In childhood we are told that our language is wrong. Repeated attacks on our native tongue diminish our sense of self" (Anzaldúa, 1999, pp. 80–81). Anzaldúa (1999) observed that hybrid languages, such as Chicano Spanish, are "not approved by any society" (p. 77). Even though students may come to school already functioning as global citizens with multilingual capacities and transnational networks with bifocality or "dual frame of reference" that enables critical thinking, their language and identities are often recast as "at-risk."

Being able to read proficiently or speak English fluently is not simply about acquiring vocabulary and grammar rules but about constructing the identity of "English speaker." Learning a new language or any other academic skill is intertwined with processes of social recognition, which include being identified by others as proficient. Learning and social recognition are not different processes, as Nielsen (2016) asserted, but "they are part of the same process" (p. 154).

"Academic notions of 'identity,'" Lave (2019) wrote,

> are no doubt over-used and under-specified . . . [yet] it is unusual to find conceptions of identity appearing in and around efforts to theorize about or carry out studies of learning. Indeed, it is rather unlikely that issues of identity (other than social labels presumed already in place), arise in studies of school learning. (p. 75)

Teachers, Lave (2109) argued, must "learn how to engage the collective identity-making (and other) relations of their students in their practices as learners learning" (p. 84). Murrell (2007) investigated how schools fostered or failed to foster collective academic identities of achievement, or what Lave (1996) called *identities of mastery*. Acquiring an identity as a successful student, both scholars maintained, is a significant dimension of schooling that involves processes of becoming, as well as social recognition from peers and teachers.

Learning the salient social divisions and identities of their social world, Lave (1996) argued, is the main task in which students engage both inside and outside the classroom: "This is an all-consuming job for children nearing adulthood, reason enough to explain why most curricular 'innovations' or teaching methods designed to improve teaching in classrooms have little effect and short lives" (p. 160). Learning is in large part about identity making and thus cannot be reduced to an SLO or turned into an isolated unit that is administratively plannable.

Technocratic research methods that analyze the individual, social activity, and material context as separate phenomena fail to help educators understand learning or "add to our understanding of what constitute processes of change in everyday life" (Nielsen, 2016, p. 156). Research that examines isolated factors, such as race, gender, or class, locates problems within individuals, as deficits of cognition, motivation, or school readiness. If researchers instead take relations as the smallest unit of analysis, they can begin to analyze learning as struggles for recognition and identity development within schools as communities of practice, rather than as a phenomenon that occurs within individuals alone.

4.4 Learning as episodic, discontinuous, and nonlinear.

Historically, educational research has sought to track learning processes based on Piaget's (1951) notion that learners move through predetermined linear stages, progressing from concrete operational thinking through abstract thought. Most instruments used in educational research rely on the assumption that time moves in a linear fashion and can be measured continuously. Learning, however, often involves leaps, setbacks, and times of redefinition (Nielsen, 1999) or reconfiguration (Barad, 2007). Learning trajectories are not linear, nor do they always obey uniform mechanisms. As Dreier (2008) argued, learning

> is mostly a discontinuous process. When a learning issue or assignment emerges for the first time for a particular person or group of persons, they encounter it in a situated way in a particular context. They address and pursue it in a particular manner in that context depending on the particular setup of materials, co-participants, and possibilities and on their particular concerns in relation to that context. (pp. 86–87)

These pursuits, Dreier (2008) added, are "rarely finished in one learning situation and context" (p. 87).

Time in research cannot be measured solely in evenly spaced moments that accurately reflect the natural chronology of events. The past, present, and future can all blend together in the classroom, as a student in any given moment can be actively remembering, perceiving, and anticipating. This jumble of activities and temporal locations happens in most instances of learning, as students apply what they have learned before in other contexts and visualize what is coming up. A teacher in an English class, for example, may be able to name when they first introduced a concept such as word order, yet this does not mark a clear beginning point for student learning. Learning is a dialogue across time, and students are always drawing on what they have learned in the past and in other contexts. As Plauborg (2018) observed, "The situations that pupils draw on . . . are entangled in a jumble of other situations and contexts, times and spaces." It is impossible to identify when the learning began: "Rather, it is the acquisition of something we already were and are a part of" (Plauborg, 2018).

It is common for educational researchers to look, for example, at interview data as a linear narrative that describes distinct time periods—retelling the past, explaining the present, or conjecturing about the future. Most researchers thus attempt to separate data neatly into disconnected spatio-temporal units. "But what if," Juelskjær (2013) asked, "we tried to think differently about what unfolds in interviews by viewing 'tellings as enactments rather than descriptions?'" (p. 760).

Time is also enfolded in the sense that what happens in the present can alter both the past (how a student remembers and narrates it) and the future (what course a student may take). Learning happens in this overlap of space-time and in leaps that cannot be tracked in a linear way. From a quantum physics perspective, as Barad (2007) suggested,

> the past is never left behind, never finished once and for all, and the future is not what will come to be in an unfolding of the present moment; rather the past and future are enfolded participants in matter's iterative becoming. (p. 234)

Learning does not commence when the teacher began a lesson or when the bell rang. When a teacher begins a lesson on dividing fractions, students are likely to already be acquainted with fractions and all the symbols related to calculation. It is not possible, then, to identify the specific time when the learning began or stopped.

In Barad's (2007) agential realism, she applied discoveries about **quantum leaps** that may help educational researchers account for the discontinuous, nonlinear nature of learning in practice. Though the phrase *quantum leap* is used in everyday speech to refer to a large movement or rapid change, in quantum physics it refers to the smallest possible change, wherein an electron "leaps" from one orbit around an atomic nucleus to another and in the process changes its energy state (Plauborg, 2018). In a quantum leap, electron movement is impossible to track or predict, as the electron "seems to disappear in one place and appear somewhere else without having been anywhere in between and without time elapsing. . . . Thus, they do not leap from one place to another, but are present in several places at once" (Plauborg, 2018). This kind of simultaneity can be used to understand students' experiences, at once within and beyond the classroom (Levitt & Schiller, 2008). "Different times and spaces," Plauborg (2018) argued, "are involved simultaneously in the learning process."

Quantum leaps can help educators describe learning processes that take into account how "something is connected and linked in new ways without it being possible to identify what has happened along the way" (Plauborg, 2018). Instead of imagining a discrete entity—a knowledge product—moving in an orderly way from one context or moment in time to another in the future, educators can reconceive of learning transfer as part of the constant ongoing activity of becoming that happens in leaps that cross and alter past, present, and future.

Even though quantum physics shows how temporality and spatiality are both "active, generative, and transformative components" (Plauborg, 2018), this agential notion of time and space is not meant to replace linear, static notions of space and time. There is no need to dispense with linear timelines, maps of classrooms, time-based observational records, or any other instruments that try to capture specific moments and places. What should be dispensed with is the notion that these instruments can reliably, validly, and fully capture all reality as it exists.

If educational researchers can open up a third space between linear/nonlinear conceptions of time and bounded/unbounded conceptions of space, it may become possible to see how the past and future are present concurrently. This is how time is handled in novels, for instance, where present action is thick with references to the past and foreshadowings of the future. The role of the narrator adds a further layer that brings other times and spaces to bear upon the protagonists as they act and speak in the perceived present.

As yet, there is little research on learning as episodic identity-building due to the constraints on educational research and the institutional pressures that enforce technocratic methods. The long-term observation involved in ethnography can provide a way to interpret changing, conflictual, and contradictory relations within learning environments, asking how they are produced in articulation with other relations across contexts. Yet traditional ethnography, since it is often mired in institutionally imposed technocratic concerns about reliability and validity, is insufficient. A more critical form of inquiry is called for that does not aim for generalizability but rather opens a third space—where researchers and learners both change and are changed by their participation. If researchers and educators can create and occupy a third space between observation and participation, they can begin to account for how the creation of an identity and learning are not separate processes but mutually constitutive, both related to changes in participation.

References

Anzaldúa, G. (1999). *Borderlands/La frontera: The new Mestiza*. Aunt Lute Press.

Appadurai, A. (1996). *Modernity at large: Cultural dimensions of globalization*. University of Minnesota Press.

Barad, K. (2007). *Meeting the universe halfway: Quantum physics and the entanglement of matter and meaning*. Duke University Press.

Barad, K. (2003). Posthumanist performativity: Toward an understanding of how matter comes to matter. *Gender and Science: New Issues, 28*(3), 801–831.

Besley, A. C. (2003). Hybridized and globalized: Youth cultures in the postmodern era. *The Review of Education, Pedagogy, and Cultural Studies, 25*(2), 153–177.

Bhabha, H. K. (1994). *The location of culture*. Routledge.

Biesta, G. J. J., & Burbules, N. C. (2003). *Pragmatism and educational research*. Rowman and Littlefield Publishers.

Christensen, G. (2016). 'Situated learning'—Beyond apprenticeship and social constructionism. In A. Qvortrup, M. Wiberg, G. Christensen, & M. Hansbøl (Eds.), *On the definition of learning* (pp. 125–140). University Press of Southern Denmark.

Clifford, J. (1988). *The predicament of culture: Twentieth-century ethnography, literature, and art*. Harvard University Press.

Colaizzi, P. (1978). Learning and existence. In R. S. Valled & M. King (Eds.), *Existential-phenomenological alternatives for psychology* (pp. 119–135). Oxford University Press.

CSU Fullerton. (2019). *Writing program learning outcomes (or goals or objectives)*. http://www.fullerton.edu/assessment/sla_resources

Dewey, J. (1910). *How we think*. Cosimo Classics.

Dewey, J. (1922). *Human nature and conduct: An introduction to social psychology*. Cosimo, Inc.

Dreier, O. (2008). Learning in structures of social practice. In S. Brinkmann, C. Elmholdt, G. Kraft, P. Musaeus, K. Nielsen, & L. Tanggaard (Eds.), *A qualitative stance: Essays in honor of Steinar Kvale* (pp. 85–96). Aarhus University Press.

Firth, A., & Wagner, J. (1997). On discourse, communication, and (some) fundamental concepts in SLA research. *The Modern Language Journal, 81*(3), 285–300.

Foucault, M. (1977). *Discipline and punish: The birth of the prison*. New York, NY: Pantheon Books.

Freire, P. (1970). *Pedagogy of the oppressed*. Continuum.

Gadamer, H. G. (1976). *Philosophical hermeneutics*. University of California Press.

Gee, J. P. (2001). Reading as situated language: A sociocognitive perspective. *Journal of Adolescent & Adult Literacy, 44*(8), 714–725.

Hall, S. (Ed.). (1996). *Representation: Cultural representations and signifying practices*. Sage Publications.

Holzkamp, K. (2013). *Psychology from the standpoint of the subject: Selected writings of Klaus Holzkamp*. Palgrave MacMillan.

Hussey, T., & Smith, P. (2002). The trouble with learning outcomes. *Active Learning in Higher Education, 3*(3), 220–233.

Juelskjær, M. (2013). Gendered subjectivities of spacetimematter. *Gender and Education, 25*(6), 754–768.

Lam, W. S. E. (2006). Border discourses and identities in transnational youth culture. In J. Mahiri (Ed.), *What they don't learn in school: Literacy in the lives of urban youth* (pp. 79–98). Peter Lang.

Lave, J. (1988). *Cognition in practice*. Cambridge University Press.

Lave, J. (1996). Teaching, as learning, in practice. *Mind, Culture, and Activity, 3*(3), 149–164.

Lave, J. (2011). *Apprenticeship in critical ethnographic practice*. University of Chicago Press.

Lave, J. (2019). *Learning and everyday life: Access, participation, and changing practice*. Cambridge University Press.

Lave, J., & McDermott, R. (2002). Estranged labor learning. *Outlines. Critical Practice Studies, 4*(1), 19–48.

Lave, J., & Wenger, E. (1991). *Situated learning: Legitimate peripheral participation*. Cambridge University Press.

Lenz Taguchi, H. (2010). *Going beyond the theory/practice divide in Early Childhood Education: Introducing an intra-active pedagogy*. Routledge.

Levitt, P., & Schiller, N. G. (2008). Conceptualizing simultaneity: A transnational social field perspective on society. In S. Khagram & P. Levitt (Eds.), *The transnational studies reader: Intersections and innovations* (pp. 284–298). Routledge.

Maira, S., & Soep, E. (Eds.). (2005). *Youthscapes: The popular, the national, and the global*. University of Pennsylvania Press.

Murrell, P. C. (2007). *Race, culture, and schooling: Identities of achievement in multicultural urban schools*. Lawrence Erlbaum Associates.

Nielsen, K. (1999). *Musical apprenticeship: Learning at the Academy of Music as socially situated*. Psychology Institute, Aarhus University.

Nielsen, K. (2006). Learning to do things with things: Apprenticeship learning in bakery as economy and social practice. In A. Costall & O. Dreier (Eds.), *Doing things with things* (pp. 209–224). Ashgate Publishing.

Nielsen, K. (2009). A collaborative perspective on learning transfer. *Journal of Workplace Learning, 21*(1), 58–70.

Nielsen, K. (2016). On defining learning from a social-ontological perspective. In A. Qvortrup, M. Wiberg, G. Christensen, & M. Hansbøl (Eds.), *On the definition of learning* (pp. 141–161). University Press of Southern Denmark.

Nielsen, K., & Kvale, S. (2006). The workplace: A landscape of learning. In E. P. Antonacopoulou, P. Jarvis, V. Andersson, S. Høyrup, & B. Elkjaer (Eds.), *Learning, working and living. Mapping the terrain of working life learning* (pp. 119–135). Palgrave Macmillan.

Piaget, J. (1951). *The psychology of intelligence*. Routledge.

Plauborg, H. (2018). Towards an agential realist concept of learning. *Subjectivity, 11*(4), 322–338.

Rasmussen, M. S. (2016). Learning from a social practice theoretical perspective. In A. Qvortrup, M. Wiberg, G. Christensen, & M. Hansbøl (Eds.). *On the definition of learning* (pp. 229–244). University Press of Southern Denmark.

Rogoff, B. (2003). *The cultural nature of human development*. Oxford University Press.

Santa Barbara City College. (2019). *Student learning outcomes*. https://www.sbcc.edu/accreditation/studentlearningoutcomes/index.php

Scribner, S., & Cole, M. (1981). *The psychology of literacy*. Harvard University Press.

Vygotsky, L. S. (1981). The instrumental method in psychology. In J. V. Wertsch (Ed.), *The concept of activity in Soviet psychology* (pp. 134–143). M. E. Sharpe.

FIVE

Expanding Third Spaces for Research

EDUCATORS ARE OVERWHELMED WITH RESEARCH findings and the responsibility of addressing individual student needs. This is not a new problem, as Dewey (1910) observed more than a century ago: "Our schools are troubled with a multiplication of studies, each in turn having its own multiplication of materials and principles. Our teachers find their tasks made heavier in that they have come to deal with pupils individually" (p. vii). The weight on teachers has only increased with the rise of high-stakes testing and mandates for student learning objectives (SLOs). Instead of trying to codify the latest best practices, this chapter looks at some ideas for how educators can open third spaces for inquiry that account for the dynamic social relations that are tied to learning.

Expanding third spaces is not meant as a new metanarrative to replace all prior approaches. Though the technocratic worldview has colonized most other forms of inquiry, no single new approach is an "uber truth that can settle all of our problems once and for all" (Biesta, 2014, p. 45). Rather, the concepts presented here are intended to help free educational researchers from such metanarratives and the binary traps that have long limited the possibilities of research practices in education and the social sciences.

5.1 Cycles of inquiry, lesson study, and archaeologies of knowledge.

In typical technocratic research practice, researchers are expected first to identify a problem and then turn it into a research question that can be operationalized. Yet social scientists, Dewey et al. (1947) argued, should never accept problems uncritically as they present themselves or be restricted to technical questions about how to solve these problems. Dewey offered a way out of the false binary between objective scientific methods and a purely subjective approach to research, arguing instead for ongoing pragmatic inquiry. The value of specific research methods, he claimed, "resides not in themselves but in their capacity to work shown in the consequences of their use" (as cited in Brinkmann, 2013, p. 76).

Dewey (1929) suggested a cycle of inquiry that is neither an isolated event nor a narrowly reactive one, in which a researcher formally defines and brackets a problem and then poses a research question that leads in linear fashion to the other stages of technocratic research design. For Dewey, inquiry is a continuous cycle that includes collecting information and generating ideas about what to do, while observing and experimenting. This cycle does not have a fixed order. Recognition of the problem, Dewey argued, may not even come first.

In Dewey's dialectical conception, the ongoing practice of inquiry includes both reflection and action. He advocated for the adoption of a "scientific attitude of mind"—an attitude similar to the "unspoiled attitude of childhood, marked by ardent curiosity, fertile imagination, and love of experimental inquiry" (Dewey, 1910, p. vii). By involving both reflection and action, there can be dual outcomes of research—not only a more specific conceptual understanding of events but also a change in practice. As Dewey argued, thinking through a problem but not doing anything about it fails to address a problematic situation. Likewise, acting without reflection, trial, and error will not add to understanding. Research as inquiry can develop what Dewey called "intelligent habits."

An example of an existing teacher professional development framework that could support educators to develop more intelligent habits is the practice of **lesson study**. An approach originally developed in Japan, lesson study encompasses a family of instructional improvement strategies, the shared feature of which is observation of classroom lessons by a group of teachers who collect and then collaboratively analyze data.

> The observed lessons, called "research lessons," are regarded not as an end in themselves but as a window on the larger vision of education shared by the group of teachers, one of whom agrees to teach the lesson while all the others make detailed records of the learning and teaching as it unfolds. These data are shared during a post-lesson colloquium, where they are used to reflect on the lesson and on learning and teaching more broadly. (Lewis et al., 2006, p. 3)

Lesson study, which is practiced in many countries, including Japan, China, Hong Kong, Singapore, and Korea, is well positioned to support teacher-driven inquiry. This kind of inquiry could, as Rorty (1991) suggested, shift research away from trying to prove one hypothesis over another toward examining the value of a hypothesis in a particular situation. In contrast to top-down mandates on implementing research-based practices, teachers engaging in lesson study research as inquiry would cycle through reflection on their own practices while experimenting with various action possibilities. Instead of accepting recommended research-based practices from administrators or consultants as the most effective (because they are based on questionably "valid and reliable" studies done elsewhere), teachers can judge their practices only after they make a change themselves and assess its consequences.

Lesson studies can also become forums for refocusing research in education on learners learning rather than on only investigating teaching and equating it with learning. In lesson studies, educators can begin to do the kind of research that Lave (2019) called for, looking at both teachers and learners as "located participant[s], and at their relations with one another (rather than at some subject-less displacement of those relations into 'instruction')" (p. 97). These investigations would need to include, then, not only learners changing ways of participating but also "the effects of teaching on teachers as learners as well" (p. 98).

Lesson study alone may not be enough, however, to examine questions of power/knowledge and how dominant norms are produced in schooling practices. Educators working together are subject to many norms that they may be unaware of, and they may fail to recognize how these norms impact their observations and evaluations. Producers and consumers of the dominant discourse—such as teachers—tend to view their own practices as standard or legitimate (Bourdieu, 1991). This view is a product of **cultural invisibility**—how those in dominant positions fail to recognize the norms of their own culture, or even that they have a culture (Rosaldo, 1989).

Supplanting the reductive cookie-cutter solutions of technocratic research with investigations that unpack specific practices and their histories, educators can extend lesson studies or other research practices to undertake Foucault's (1972, 1973) **archaeologies of knowledge**. Foucault's approach to inquiry deconstructs the origins of dominant discursive structures. His premise is that **discourses**—systems of knowledge, language, and power—are governed by social and ideological rules beyond grammar or logic. Through his archaeology, Foucault unpacked how "certain texts and storylines get monumentalized into dominant narratives that become authoritative 'history'" (Weems, 2004, pp. 227–228).

Foucault used the term *discourse* to refer to dominant narratives and, more broadly, to academic disciplines, fields of interest, or other large codified bodies of knowledge, such as early childhood education, second language acquisition, and special education. The formation of discourses is embedded in "a complex group of relations that function as a rule" (Foucault, 1972, p. 74), delineating regularities of inclusion and exclusion, of possibility and foreclosure. He described discourses "as practices that systematically form the objects of which they speak" (Foucault, 1972, p. 49). Or as Ball (1990) put it, discourses are "about what can be said, and thought, but also about who can speak, when, where and with what authority" (p. 17).

Discourses deserve to be analyzed, Foucault (1972) argued, because "they are not intrinsic . . . and universally recognized characteristics" but are contingent upon power relations (p. 22). For Foucault (1972), the central question is "How is it that one particular statement or form of knowledge appeared rather than another" (p. 27). He sought through his archaeologies of knowledge to examine a phenomenon "in the exact specificity of its occurrence; determine its conditions of existence, fix at least its limits, establish its correlations with other statements that may be connected with it, and show what other forms of statement it excludes" (Foucault, 1972, p. 28).

In his historical investigations of the discourses of multiple institutions, Foucault deconstructed the roots of madness (2006), illness (1973), discipline and punishment (1977), and sexuality (1990). In *History of Madness*, for example, Foucault (2006) excavated the different discourses that have governed talk and thought about sanity and madness. In each of these works, he showed how bodies of knowledge are historically contingent, rather than universal truths. As he observed, "We must question those ready-made syntheses, those groupings that we normally accept before any examination, those links whose validity is recognized from the outset" (Foucault, 1972, p. 22).

All discourses have had different meanings at different points in history, and these meanings shift constantly—and often abruptly. Foucault argued, similar to Kuhn's (1969) notion of revolutionary paradigm shifts, that discourses emerge and transform not according to a smoothly developing series of common worldviews but by breaks and ruptures. Foucault suggested that the concepts of discontinuity, fragmentation, and transformation present particularly promising avenues of inquiry. An archaeology of knowledge depends on deconstructing normalized continuities.

In one example of an archaeology of knowledge, Coloma (2009) charted the transnational history of race, empire, and curriculum in the colonial educational system of the Philippines under U.S. rule in the early 1900s. Coloma traced the discourse in popular and official representations that depicted colonized Filipino/as as racially Black. He illustrated the discursive effects on educational policy and curriculum in the Philippines, showing how the schooling for African Americans in the U.S. South served as the template for pedagogy in the Philippines. The discursive construction of Filipino/as not only reveals the pervasiveness of White supremacist views in U.S. domestic and colonial spheres, but also shows how the discourse of White supremacy set into motion a segmented educational program that initiated and perpetuated sociocultural and economic disparities: "The tension between academic and manual-industrial instruction became a site of convergence for Filipino/as and African Americans, with decided implications for the lived trajectories in stratified racialized and colonized communities" (Coloma, 2009, p. 495). How those in power construe racialized and colonized Others indelibly shapes the type of education provided to them.

Besley (2003) also conducted an archaeology of knowledge to challenge dominant discourses and assumptions about the categories of adolescence and youth more broadly, considering how this age group is constructed and positioned in education. Besley found that most of the discourse on youth in the "psy" sciences (psychology, psychoanalysis, clinical psychology, social work, psychotherapy, counseling) is problematic in its labeling and stigmatizing of young people. She critiqued the category of "adolescence" as a reflection of a Western behaviorist psychology "that largely ignores its own power/knowledge" (Besley, 2003, p. 154). Following the flawed but tacitly accepted "storm and stress" model of adolescence—a developmental stage said to be marked by conflict with parents, risky behavior, and mood disruptions (G. S. Hall, 1931)—schools institute comprehensive surveillance and disciplinary measures that assign blame directly on youth and their hormones. These structures further normalize and perpetuate the criminalization of youth without any recognition that the storm and stress model is a historical and cultural production, rather than a universal given.

Besley (2003) examined how market forces and discourses of consumerism shape globalized, hybrid youth identities: "The market infiltrates the social fabric, shaping young market populations in the habits and disciplines of consumerism" (p. 165). Youth identities may feel unique given the broad range of choices in the marketplace, but they reflect specific limits set by the kinds of products available and the practices and values of consumerism. As Besley argued,

> Kids assemble their identities in the global marketplace on the basis of what their local culture predisposes them to make. They make individual choices that are reinforced by market logic that creates them as niche markets that . . . has the effect of manufacturing, legitimating, and then exploiting their identities/subjectivities. (p. 168)

Foucault's archaeologies of knowledge can be used to show how discursive norms shape and limit action possibilities. Institutions such as schools exercise power through discourse, and problematic patterns are maintained because they seem natural and plausible. Archaeologies of knowledge can reduce cultural invisibility, making the familiar unfamiliar and challenging taken-for-granted notions. If educators can employ research as inquiry and conduct archaeologies of knowledge as part of their practice, then they may be able to develop more intelligent habits, recognizing and disrupting the norms that produce inequities.

5.2 Multivocal narratives as third spaces.

Instead of deploying technocratic methods to produce valid and reliable studies, educational researchers can seek to collect, craft, and share narratives—stories that provide perspective and concrete specifics. Though discredited in comparison to "scientific" reports, narratives can reduce cultural invisibility, enabling researchers to see from viewpoints other than their own. The medium of narratives is also well suited for collecting, analyzing, and articulating contextualized and complex data. While narratives readily convey situated perspectives, they offer far more than unique first-person subjective accounts. They can also operate as discursive third spaces for articulating simultaneity and multiple, shifting positionalities. Unlike technocratic research reporting, narratives allow for layered, multivocal views on local knowledge and practice, and they offer concrete specifics while remaining open to further interpretation (Canagarajah, 1996).

Narratives are not entirely absent from contemporary social science research practice. The field of **narrative inquiry** is considered a legitimate, if marginalized, form of research. Under the technocratic framework, narratives are viewed as a potentially valid form of data. Yet this domestication of narrative emphasizes gathering the stories of individuals as coherent texts that have inherent validity and analyzing them according to prescribed coding practices to ensure reliability. Technocratic researchers believe that collected narratives can represent holistically the experiences of individuals and generate a valid depiction of them. This interpretation of narratives reduces their potential as a means to open third spaces.

The paradigm of **critical race theory** (CRT), in contrast, recognizes the power of narratives as a way of demonstrating power and positionality in the context of racial identity (Delgado & Stefancic, 2017) or migratory status (Pérez Huber, 2020). CRT scholars argue that counterstorytelling, also referred to as *testimonio*, legitimizes the narratives of marginalized people while offering alternatives to dominant narratives (Bell, 1987; Dixson & Rousseau, 2005; Ladson-Billings & Tate, 2016). Originally based upon work from the field of legal studies, CRT scholars articulate five themes: the intercentricity of race and racism with other forms of subordination, a challenge to dominant ideology, commitment to social justice, the centrality of experiential knowledge and lived experience, and a transdisciplinary perspective (Solórzano & Delgado Bernal, 2001; Yosso, 2005). These scholars advocate drawing directly on the lived experiences of people "by including such methods as storytelling, family histories, biographies, scenarios, parables, *cuentos*, *testimonios*, chronicles and narratives" (Yosso, 2005, p. 74).

The term *voice* is prevalent in CRT discourse in a way that is meant to legitimize the experiential knowledge of all people—particularly those who are marginalized. CRT scholars employ personal narratives and other stories to interrogate technocratic and White supremacist approaches, which often characterize discrimination (or its "absence") narrowly and incompletely. A goal of such "voice scholarship" is to subvert dominant narratives and realities and foster transformational resistance (Solórzano & Delgado Bernal, 2001). Narratives can also document overlooked racial microaggressions—the "subtle, innocuous, preconscious, or unconscious degradations, and put-downs" based on race that over a lifetime can "contribute to diminished mortality, augmented morbidity, and flattened confidence" (Sue, 2004, p. 767; Yosso et al., 2009, p. 661).

Narratives have the possibility of expressing complexity and exploring the hybrid possibilities of **intersectionality**, a perspective that draws attention to the simultaneous and interacting effects of gender, race, class, sexual orientation, language, and national origin as overlapping categories of difference. Technocratic educational research often relies on collapsing identity into single reductive categories of race, class, and gender. These narrow one-dimensional conceptualizations of identity, Crenshaw (1991) argued, "fail to transcend difference [and] . . . frequently conflate or ignore intragroup differences. . . . Moreover, ignoring difference within groups contributes to tension among groups" (p. 142). Emerging over the past two decades as an explicitly interdisciplinary approach, Hancock (2007) noted, "intersectionality considers the interaction of such categories as organizing structures of society, recognizing that these key components influence political access, equality, and the potential for any form of justice" (p. 64).

Narratives provide a forum for addressing the ways identities are cross-cut, allowing for recognition of the intersectional positions that many people occupy between codified categories of race, class, and gender. Through the concreteness of narratives, it is possible to display the kinds of belonging and not belonging that can occur simultaneously, the ways it is possible to be "both/and" or "outsiders within." "Telling stories," Holvino (2008) argued,

> and articulating the narratives of organizational actors across different axes of power and identity practices is an important intervention for changing dominant organizational discourses because it brings to light alternative narratives that seldom find their way into mainstream accounts and organizational mythologies . . . [and they can] help change the experience that organizational members have across dimensions of difference from that of a "generalized other" to a "concrete other." (p. 16)

Tuhiwai Smith (1999) identified narratives and storytelling as a powerful research tool, not because narratives offer a unique valid account but because they offer complex multiple perspectives:

> Each individual story is powerful. But the point about the stories is not that they simply tell a story, or tell a story simply. These new stories contribute to a collective story . . . a way of representing the "diversities of truth" within which the storyteller rather than the researcher retains control . . . Intrinsic in storytelling is a focus on dialogue and conversations. (pp. 144–145)

Unlike most technocratic research reports, narratives—along with oral histories and forms of popular culture—allow for a dialogue of multiple voices. Bakhtin (1981) referred to the multivocality of narratives and their layering of viewpoints as **heteroglossia.** Bakhtin showed how narratives are premised on a "the diversity of speech and not the unity of a normative shared language" (p. 308). He analyzed cultural products that defy official, unitary, or authoritative monologues, particularly the medieval European carnival tradition in the works of Chaucer or Baudelaire, and polyphonic novels, such as those of Dostoevsky. He showed how these works are all dialogic. "What Dostoevsky's characters *say,*" wrote Bakhtin, "constitutes an arena of never-ending struggle with others' words. . . . For this reason these utterances may serve as excellent models of the most varied forms for transmitting and framing another's discourse" (p. 349).

Bakhtin (1981) suggested that narratives and other forms of popular culture can give voice to unofficial ways of talking about the world that challenge the monologue of official or dominant professions, classes, or interests:

> Heteroglossia, once incorporated into the novel . . . is *another's speech in another's language*, serving to express authorial intentions but in a refracted way. Such speech constitutes a special type of *double-voiced discourse.* It serves two speakers at the same time and expresses simultaneously two different intentions: the direct intention of the character who is speaking, and the refracted intention of the author. . . . A potential dialogue is embedded in them. (p. 40)

In contrast to researchers, who often try to make their language seem neutral and objective, novelists do not strip away the social intentions behind their words. Nor do novelists attempt to remove specific contexts in order to form generalizations. As Bakhtin observed, "The internal social dialogism of novelistic discourse requires the concrete social context to be exposed . . . ; for indeed, social dialogue reverberates in all aspects of discourse, in those relating to 'content' as well as the 'formal' aspects themselves" (p. 300).

Few if any "neutral, hard elements ('rock bottom truths')" within a novel are "not drawn into dialogue" (Bakhtin, 1981, p. 300). Through their inclusion of multiple voices, narratives can contain a "multiplicity of 'language' and verbal-ideological belief systems" (Bakhtin, 1981, p. 311). Though these incorporated languages always refract the author's intentions, they can also expose the rationalities of each speaker. "In every case," Bakhtin (1981) argued

> a particular belief system belonging to someone else, a particular point of view on the world belonging to someone else, is used by the author because it is highly productive, . . . it is able on the one hand to show the object of representation in a new light . . . and on the other hand to illuminate in a new way the "expected" literary horizon. (p. 313)

Bakhtin's concept of heteroglossia also articulates the primary importance of context. No utterance can be understood if it is divorced from the conditions—material, social, historical—in which it is expressed. A word said in one context will invariably have a different meaning when expressed in a different time and place. This capacity for inclusion of multiple viewpoints, simultaneity, and contingencies makes narratives far more useful than secondary source material that presents educators with abstract, reductive findings, such as "Research shows X to be the most effective way to improve Y."

In his ethnographic work "Deep Play: Notes on the Balinese Cockfight," Geertz (1973) presented a narrative of a Balinese cockfighting event, showing how this brutal ritual symbolically "provides a metasocial commentary upon the whole matter of assorting human beings into fixed hierarchical ranks and then organizing the major part of collective existence around that assortment" (p. 448). While Geertz's narrative tries to make Balinese customs comprehensible to readers, it is not valuable because it offers an authoritative account, but because it engages readers in a dialogue with the events and opens up possible interpretations. As Geertz observed, "The cockfight is not the master key to Balinese life, any more than bullfighting is to Spanish. What it says about life is not unqualified nor even unchallenged by what other equally eloquent cultural statements say about it" (p. 452). Geertz's narrative offers possibilities for decoding how positionality and power emerge in a specific context.

Ethnographic narratives in educational research can likewise be valuable to educators, not because they can validly capture a community for all time, but because they provide space for the researcher to make visible the shifting dynamics of power and positioning. As Khawaja and Mørck (2009) argued, "A focus on positioning, power relations, processes of becoming, and social construction calls for research methods that capture the complexity, ambiguity, and multiplicity of the social reality of the subject" (p. 31). Narratives, such as the following one from an elementary school Back-to-School night, can capture the complex ways in which material conditions and discursive norms are entangled:

> *Back-to-School night:* A table is set up in the multi-purpose room with coffee, sugar, and cookies for the families. A classroom assistant stands behind the table to help serve. A mother approaches the table shyly, says "hello," the one word of English she knows, and starts to pile cookies on her paper plate. "You can only take one," says the teacher. Understanding only the stern tone of voice, the mother hesitates and glances around the room. "You can only take one," repeats the teacher, holding up a single finger, "Just one. We have lots of parents to serve." The mother begins to put the cookies back, eyes on the floor. "No, no. You can't do that now that you've touched them," says the teacher, shaking her head. The mother shrinks away from the table with a single cookie. She moves to the back corner of the room where a few families sit together and she breaks off pieces of the cookie to share with each of her children and their cousins. Her daughter watches as the teacher tosses the rest of the pile into the trash. (Blakely, 2007, p. 78)

Such narratives can become starting places for collaborative reflection on moments of tension and conflicting norms, and they can serve as vehicles to help educators generate new possible lines of action.

Not only do narratives allow for simultaneity in intersectional processes of becoming, they also allow for simultaneity of past, present, and future. Narratives can relate within a moment the unpredictable connections their protagonists may make to the past, present, or future. By gaining access to protagonists' thoughts, readers can see the present unfold, layered with memories about what already happened or worries about what has yet to happen. Narratives provide a forum for chronologically interwoven moments of recalling, encountering, and anticipating.

Use of narrative can challenge, too, the linear notion of research in conventional research reporting, offering a more complex account of the research process. Unlike traditional third-person methodology reports of how data were collected and analyzed, narratives can present the messier, discontinuous ways that research unfolds, capturing contradictions, dilemmas, wrong turns, and unexpected discoveries. As Marzano (2007) observed, "The autobiographical accounts of their research experiences frequently published by ethnographers are full of narratives about false starts, scrapped projects, and illuminating discoveries made in the field, often by chance and which move the research in an entirely unexpected direction" (p. 429). Missteps and dilemmas are often excluded from Methods sections, though they may inform other researchers who will similarly encounter dilemmas, tensions, and unexpected events in their work.

5.3 Crossing contexts and moving into borderlands.

Crossing contexts—moving across physical spaces and between communities—can also help reduce cultural invisibility and open up possibilities for dialogue and interpretation. Crossing contexts makes visible prearranged routines and standard practices, whereas moving into or deliberately generating borderlands can help suspend, combine, or remake those norms; expand possible lines of action; and provide productive sites for reflection (Rosaldo, 1989). It is in these in-between spaces, Nielsen (2009) argued, where there is the most potential: "The boundary zone is a place where reflections and new suggestions can be put forth" (p. 67).

Shadowing students, teachers, or administrators throughout their day, as they move from home to school and out into the community, can provide perspective that is impossible to see in only one location (Wolcott, 1973). In one Northern California school, for example, a new principal decided to shadow a few students to get to know the school community before his official start date. Following students from their apartment complex onto the bus, to the cafeteria for breakfast, and then to the hallway, waiting for the first period bell to ring, the principal gained perspective on some of the school's historic discipline problems. Instead of implementing stricter discipline measures, as teachers had initially recommended, he advocated to change the school's bus route and bell schedule to reduce the long wait times students experienced. When these changes were implemented, there was an immediate reduction in the number of incidents reported to his office every morning. Shadowing or other forms of crossing contexts allow educators to see how "subjects, objects, lives, and worlds are made in their relations" across practices (Lave, 2011, p. 152).

Dreier (2008) argued that only by crossing contexts can researchers begin to investigate learning, for learning does not happen at one time, in one place:

> Learners are not stationary. Being situated does not mean staying in the same place. Indeed, in social practice learners are moving, and these moves play a key role in their accomplishment of learning. The very course of learning processes is grounded in learners' movements in social practice. (p. 86)

Since learning is episodic and discontinuous, researching it requires crossing contexts. Comparing across contexts may, in turn, lead to more complex understandings (Dreier, 2008).

Heath's (1982, 1983) ethnographies of language and literacy practices in three communities in the Southeastern United States provide an example of how moving across contexts and following different students from their homes and neighborhoods into the classroom can illustrate ongoing processes of language socialization and their embedded power relations. In her study of three communities—Maintown: a middle-class school-oriented community; Roadville: a low-income White Appalachian mill community; and Trackton: a rural, low-income Black community—Heath challenged reductive binaries (Black/White and oral/literate traditions) that define thinking about so-called at-risk students. She resisted the presumption of preexisting bounded social categories, along with the homogeneous groupings of race usually displayed in educational research. After following students across many settings from home to school, she discovered that

> ascribing Black, Southern, or Standard English to speakers by racial membership was not satisfactory to these students, for almost all of them could shift among these varieties as occasion demanded. To categorize children and their families on the basis of either socioeconomic class or race and then to link these categories to discrete language differences was to ignore the realities of the communicative patterns of the region. (Heath, 1983, p. 3)

Heath (1983) described the different storytelling practices students inherited from their families and communities. In Roadville, stories had to be invited or announced by another group member, whereas in Trackton, storytellers competed to insert their story into the dialogue, adding dramatic gestures, imitations of voices, and sound effects to entertain their audience. "True stories" in Trackton are full of exaggerations, and storytellers are well versed in "talkin' junk." "In short," wrote Heath, "for Roadville, Trackton's stories would be lies; for Trackton, Roadville's stories would not even count as stories" (p. 189).

Stories in Maintown, in contrast, were generally organized chronologically with a clear beginning, middle, and end. Their stories tended to be topic focused, about a single person or event, and thus they matched mainstream teacher expectations. Maintown children learned to "talk like a book" at home. When there is a congruence between a student's language use and the demands of educational settings, then, Bourdieu (1991) argued, they are able to "reap symbolic benefits by speaking in a way that comes naturally to them" (p. 21). Such literate discourse styles "are not more or less effective for communicating or organizing thought than the styles used by other groups," Rogoff (2003) contended, "but they facilitate success in schools that use the same structures" (p. 303; Labov, 1972).

While crossing contexts can help reduce the cultural invisibility that leads educators, for example, to believe there is one universal way of telling stories, this practice alone may be insufficient for expanding possibilities for dialogue, interpretation, and new lines of action. Intentionally developing material third spaces—configuring physical locations that support interactions—can help different communities cross contexts and suspend norms that have historically excluded certain kinds of participation. For example, teachers in one U.S. school created a third space or boundary zone between home and school by transforming the school's multipurpose room into a café-like setting for parent–teacher meetings (Blakely, 2007).

Following the model of "World Café" (Brown et al., 2005), school staff brought in small tables decorated with tablecloths, flowers, and candles. This change in the material arrangements of the space visibly shifted the dynamics of parent–teacher relations. Instead of sitting in forward-facing fold-out chairs with staff and parents in different rows and the principal above them at the podium, the parents, teachers, and administrators now sat mixed together in small groups on the same level. Moving from the role of passive recipients of announcements, with a few vocal parent leaders coming up to take the microphone, all the parents now had more informal conversations with administrators and teachers.

The monthly café meetings became key sites for collaborative learning and catalysts for change in the community. After many conversations between staff and parents, the school's focus for grant writing and fundraising shifted from supporting additional counseling services, which teachers had thought was the priority, to supporting more enrichment and after-school programs. Parent attendance increased exponentially at each café dinner; there was also an increase in attendance from new community members, local nonprofits, school board administrators, and other neighborhood schools. Attendance diminished immediately, however, when administrators, concerned over the costs of childcare for younger siblings at the well-attended café-style meetings, changed the evening meeting time, took away the potluck dinner, and removed the café furnishings. The boundary zone created through the material arrangements of the café that were key to the community's engagement had disappeared, and community participation disappeared along with it.

Although material arrangements such as the World Café can be agential in creating third spaces, simply setting up physical boundary zones alone without deliberate facilitation may not lead to collaborative learning. In Nielsen's (2006) interviews in bakeries and vocational schools, he found that there were often missed learning opportunities because the masters or journeymen at the bakeries did not facilitate any boundary crossing when apprentices and experienced bakers were set up to work together. In many situations, the masters or journeymen kept their distance from the apprentices, such as when the master took the recipe into his office and solved the production problems himself or when the journeymen threw out a failed product instead of inviting the apprentices to use what they had learned in school to evaluate what went wrong. When spaces for collaborative learning were deliberately created, Nielsen found that they were beneficial to both sides. Apprentices were able to discuss the theories they were learning concurrently in school, which helped them to realize that their classroom training had utility. It also helped journeymen to reflect on their own knowledge and to generate new ways to solve problems.

Doing research in a deliberately collaborative way that blurs the lines between masters and apprentices, researchers and subjects, school and home, or school and workplace requires ongoing redesign and evaluation of the research process. **Participatory research** (also called participatory action research) offers a way for researchers to open third spaces deliberately by blurring the line between researchers and research subjects. Participatory research was initially developed in Africa and Latin America and subsequently appropriated in the United States and Europe. It blends community participation in all aspects of decision-making and implementation of research studies.

A participatory research perspective, asserted B. L. Hall (2005), postulates that most technocratic research is conducted and funded through hierarchical structures that ask questions from a top-down perspective, focusing problem formulation, analysis, and knowledge creation on the researcher—and not on the people or communities being researched. Instead, participatory research is meant to be of immediate and direct benefit to a community, as it involves community members in the entire project from problem formulation, to data collection and analysis, to conclusion and action on findings. The aim is to establish community needs and increase awareness and commitment in communities, as a dialectical process over time—not as a static picture from one point in time.

Participatory research is occasionally presented briefly in research methods texts and university courses, though mostly in reductive accounts and applications. Technocratic researchers seldom go beyond **member checking**, a validation technique that asks participants to check findings for accuracy, in their attempts to introduce a participatory dimension to their studies. Participant involvement in data analysis is used at most as a tool for triangulation to build validity. This application domesticates participatory research by failing to recognize how the paradigm is meant to overturn and recast power relations between researchers and their subjects. Torre and Fine (2006) and Akom (2009) employ participatory research with youth communities in particular, terming it youth participatory action research (YPAR). As described by Akom, YPAR is

> a collaborative approach that breaks down the barriers between the researcher and the researched and values community members as equitable partners in the research enterprise, . . . underscor[ing] the liberatory principles of agency, equity, and self-determination. . . . [It] identifies research as a significant site of struggle between the . . . ways of knowing of traditional Western research and decolonizing frameworks . . . to accurately assess our own strengths and needs and our right to act upon them. (p. 513)

YPAR projects often center around issues of structural violence that impact the lives of young people, including educational justice, health care, criminalization and police oppression of youth, gentrification, and environmental issues. Akom suggested that YPAR represents an orientation to inquiry that is closely consistent with the principles of CRT. By engaging research "subjects" as active participants in all phases of research studies (Akom, 2009; Fals-Borda, 1987; B. L. Hall, 2005; Torre & Fine, 2006), participatory research and YPAR go well beyond member checking.

A Scandinavian research approach, termed **practice research**, also seeks to cross contexts and enroll research participants more actively in the research process (Mørck & Huniche, 2006). Based on critical psychology (Holzkamp, 2013) and social practice theory (Mørck & Huniche, 2006), the goal of practice research is "to unfold social self-understandings" in practice with as much detail as possible and "to work through these social self-understandings in cooperation with the participants as co-researchers" (Kristensen & Mørck, 2016, p. 4). In Kristensen and Mørck's research following a first grader, for example, the researchers looked at how school discourses around attention-deficit/hyperactivity disorder and its medicalization contribute to the student feeling like a troublemaker at home and at school, stuck with the "un-resolvable conundrum" that he must, as he said, "behave differently from myself" (p. 8). The student's parents feel trapped between the choice of medicating their son (who does not like the tired, numb feeling he has on the prescribed drug) or risking his alienation at school (because his peers and teachers are so frustrated with his disruptions). The researchers create a space to discuss the dilemma with the students and classroom teachers, helping them recognize the limits of the binary choice for the student between being "drugged into normality and passivity" or ostracized (Kristensen & Mørck, 2016, p. 9). Together, they examine photographs taken during the school day and discuss their reasons for action at various moments. In the process, they come to some "practice recognitions," including the student's realization that he is not alone in struggling to stay still during lessons and the teacher's understanding of how the enforcement of strict rules creates a class culture of scrutinizing and picking on each other. From these practice recognitions, they begin to imagine new action possibilities.

Unlike most social science research that tries to minimize the researchers' involvement to reduce bias and maintain a false sense of objectivity, practice researchers are actively involved in changing the forms and trajectories of participation: It "is a way of practicing research that is characterized by active involvement with practice, becoming part of the often contentious field being researched" (Mørck & Huniche, 2006, pp. 12–13). Practice research studies often involve enrolling coresearchers as active participants in both the goal setting and content of the research, as well as in the analysis and write-up of the findings (Mørck & Huniche, 2006, p. 13).

Enrolling co-researchers or doing any kind of participatory research requires "continual brokering from boundary positions, that is, 'walking the margins'" of established positions, negotiating, and legitimizing new ones (Mørck, 2010, p. 189). Recognizing complex power imbalances between researchers and coresearchers or research subjects is inevitably part of doing this kind of participatory work. Part of developing research practices needs to involve, then, not only enrolling research subjects or co-researchers, but also creating democratic spaces to explore how researcher positioning impacts the community. Researchers and co-researchers can use their own third space to: navigate the ethical dilemmas and processes of othering that are inevitably a part of the research; explore contradictions and reckon with the double binds that researchers may be in, such as feeling trapped between being considered an informer or untrustworthy; and expand action possibilities across the community. In such third spaces, it becomes possible to straddle cultural divides or self/Other binaries and occupy multiple positions at once, learning how to talk about "'being both,' speaking within two or more conflicting practice ideologies at the same time, without correcting or censuring" (Mørck, 2011, p. 131).

Shadowing and crossing contexts can help educational researchers investigate the situated practices of learners. Yet, observing different students in the classroom and then simply tacking on other settings—following them to the park or visiting them at home—is insufficient. The goal of crossing contexts is not to make comparisons or improve the validity of research studies through triangulation. The point of comparing or crossing contexts is to help researchers critique their own practices and the norms they take for granted and to become more aware of the relations that produce them. Such recognition of cultural invisibility requires both crossing contexts and opening third spaces that enable researchers to see how their own changing practices shape—and are shaped by—the practices they investigate.

5.4 Supporting democracy and imagination in research forums.

The best community configuration for developing research practices, Dewey suggested, is a democratic one. He argued that this is the only form flexible enough to support inquiry in ever-changing communities. For Dewey, democracy is not just a political system but a culture or "form of life . . . that best positions us to respond collectively to those challenges that we necessarily encounter in a changeable world" (Brinkmann, 2013, p. 134). By expanding or repurposing the structures already in place for teacher preparation and collaboration, educators can begin to develop democratic forums for decision-making and cultivate the imagination and empathy necessary for doing research responsively and ethically.

Many countries, including the United States, have infrastructure in place that could be repurposed as democratic research forums to help educators open third spaces for inquiry. A range of partnership-based, collaborative teacher professional development models already exist in multiple countries, including Great Britain (Hargreaves & Shirley, 2009), Finland (Sahlberg, 2007, 2011), and China (Guo et al., 2013); these could be leveraged to support more democratic forums for teacher inquiry. One of these frameworks—**professional learning communities** (PLC)—is widely applied in the United States and elsewhere for professional development activities. The term PLC can be amorphous, describing many combinations of individuals with an interest in education—a grade-level teaching team, a school committee, a high school department, an entire school district, a state department of education, a national professional organization, or networks of schools and agencies (DuFour, 2004). In the current neoliberal climate, PLCs often focus on narrow top-down activities such as "writing PLOs" or "teaching to standards." Yet it is possible to repurpose this concept to support communities of practice for teachers to plan and conduct their own inquiries into topics that are of direct concern to them.

Repurposed PLCs can serve not only as a space for local inquiry practices but also as a vehicle for sharing experience across communities. One way to disseminate knowledge through relationships is via existing networks not only within schools but among them. As Hargreaves and Shirley (2009) reported,

> Teachers and schools learn best not by reading research reports, listening to speeches, or attending workshops, but by watching, listening to, and learning from each other. . . . When making change, it is . . . important to build new relationships among people engaged in practice together. (p. 99)

Participation in such networks needs to be invited rather than compulsory. Governments or foundations can help initiate and fund the networks but not interfere in them or use them to evaluate and rank schools. Only then can experiential knowledge be "circulated among respected practitioners" (Hargreaves & Shirley, 2009, p. 100).

Democratic forums within schools, however, such as lesson study, may be insufficient in addressing systemic racism and other institutional norms that are culturally invisible. Only when educators cross contexts can they gain perspective on normalized forms of racism, for example, as well as have spaces to facilitate dialogue with other community members, professionals, and scholars.

Collaborative structures to support opening third spaces for inquiry, for instance, already exist between universities and K-12 schools. Most universities that prepare K-12 teachers have established relationships with surrounding school districts or agencies to place student teachers in classrooms for practical teacher experience. University faculty build relationships with teachers, often provide professional development support, and share responsibility for supervising and helping student teachers develop as professionals. If its paradigm were shifted, then this widespread infrastructure could expand third spaces for inquiry.

Another existing framework for supporting third space expansion is **research–practice partnerships** (RPPs): "RPPs are long-term collaborations between practitioners and researchers that are organized to investigate problems of practice" (Coburn & Penuel, 2016, p. 48). Because of the perceived success of high-profile RPPs such as the University of Chicago Consortium for Chicago School Research, the Strategic Education Research Partnership, the Carnegie Foundation's Networked Improvement Communities, and others, funders are investing resources to support expansion. The challenge for employing this model would be to interrogate and shift power relationships in order to enable educators to drive research agendas and avoid the technocratic aims and top-down initiatives that often characterize university–school relationships and foundation-funded initiatives.

In addition to supporting more democratic processes for inquiry, research cohorts or repurposed PLCs and RPPs can help researchers to develop and apply imagination to their work. There is no place in technocratic research methodology instruction for creative work or activities that cultivate imagination; in the scientistic paradigm, the humanities and imagination in general are devalued and seen as lacking rigor. Yet, Dewey (1925) argued, "Every great advance in science has issued from a new audacity of imagination" (p. 310; see also Dewey, 1916/1966). Though it has disappeared from the neoliberal discourse of educational agencies worldwide (the European Commission, Organisation for Economic Co-operation and Development, and U.S. Department of Education)—replaced with a discourse of "training and basic skills"—imagination remains a crucial part of how meaning, knowledge, and decisions are made (d'Agnese, 2017).

By imagination, Dewey (1934) did not refer to its common definition as the generation of fantasy or unreality, but as a crucial element that supplements and deepens observation. Imagination, he argued, is "the medium of realization of every kind of thing which lies beyond the scope of direct physical response" (p. 277). Understanding any interaction requires recovering meanings from prior experiences and projecting possible meanings in the future: "Imagination is the only gateway through which these meanings can find their way into a present interaction; or, rather" (Dewey, 1934, p. 272). Imagination is "the junction at which (a) we can pass from activity to knowledge and (b) we can pass from symbols to meanings" (d'Agnese, 2017, p. 444).

Willis (2000) argued that imagination is a crucial element in evoking phenomenon: "The problem with empirical data, empirically presented, is that they can be flat and uninteresting, a documentary of detail which does not connect with urgent issues. . . . [W]ell-grounded and illuminating analytic points flow only from . . . the ethnographic imagination" (p. xi).

To illuminate urgent issues, researchers need expanded third spaces that exist between the established binaries of objective/subjective or expository/creative writing. Willis (2000) contended that "good ethnographic writing" is achieved not through "ever extended techniques of validity" but through creative work that "shows the complexities of lived relations and forms for which words and theories do not yet exist" (pp. 118–119).

Imagination enables researchers to think through possible futures and consequences of specific actions. It is pivotal, too, in doing research ethically. Instead of authoritarian bodies that supply a one-time stamp of approval for proposed research, democratic forums could work collaboratively to navigate situation-specific ethical dilemmas on an ongoing basis. Rather than wasting energy on helping students overcome bureaucratic hurdles in the institutional review board process, faculty advisors could share cases, narratives, and images of research situations, discussing ethical dilemmas and working together to imagine new lines of action. Far more substantially than textbook checklists of ethical dos and don'ts, role-playing and other imaginative work can shift perspectives to build empathy. Greene (1995) suggested, too, that imagination helps individuals "look at things as if they could be otherwise" (p. 16).

Research cohorts can serve not only as democratic forums where faculty and students make collaborative decisions, they can also become sites for researchers to invite study participants to become co-researchers. These participatory forums can be the starting point for participants to become actively involved in all aspects of the research in their communities. Democratic research forums can review not only the ethics behind a study's design but also the kinds of research topics that are selected, who gets to conduct research, how data are analyzed, and how findings are disseminated. This would integrate ethical review more broadly into the full range of research practices and begin to undo the legacy of scientistic research that maintains significant power imbalances between researchers and their subjects.

5.5 Research as an entangled material-discursive practice.

Democratic research forums can help educational researchers acknowledge and inquire about the constantly changing forms of learner participation, as well as how researchers themselves can learn and change in relation to their research. Technocratic researchers, seeking to maintain objectivity, remove themselves from their findings. In their efforts to control threats to internal validity and reduce bias, they edit out their own perspectives, the impacts they may have on the research participants, and the impacts the research may have on them. Technocratic researchers continue to rely on the Newtonian physics of the 17th century, assuming that they can capture a stable reality "out there" and test their hypotheses in a valid and reliable manner to determine what causes learning outcomes. Barad (2007) argued, instead following quantum physics, that phenomena are not things that have a fixed impact or outcome but relations that are constantly reconfiguring. She argued further against the idea that it is only humans who have agency to impact practices; she maintained that material forces are also agential.

From her agential realist perspective, material arrangements (of objects) and discursive practices (of subjects) cannot be separated; they are entangled (Barad, 2007). "To be entangled is not simply to be intertwined with another, as in the joining of separate entities, but to lack an independent, self-contained existence. Existence is not an individual affair" (Barad, 2007, p. 9). Blurring the distinction between subjects and objects, Barad (2007) argued that there are no preexisting internal mental states (motivated/unmotivated, attentive/distracted, cooperative/oppositional) or other properties (race, gender, class) that can be assigned to individuals and made available for research. There are, for example, no bullies or at-risk readers or low-income students in an abstract sense; rather, there are complex conditions that produce bullying, failure, racism, sexism, and poverty. Thus, educational researchers can shift away from trying to identify which independent variable leads to which learning outcome and instead examine how material-discursive practices co-produce relations and how these relations are entangled across contexts.

Applying the concept of material-discursive entanglement in an educational context, Lenz Taguchi (2010) argued that "the learner and the world cannot be separated, but are of the world in a co-dependency" (p. 47). Lenz Taguchi's story about the first day of school illustrates the entanglement of material spaces, pedagogical concepts and norms, gendered subjectivities, and the way they are constituted and made meaningful in the processes of learning and becoming learners:

> On my first day of preschool the teacher took all of us into the large and light playroom. She told us to sit down on an assigned dot glued to the floor. The dots formed a large circle and by the main wall there was a soft red pillow where the teacher seated herself crossing her legs in front of her, telling us to do the same. I could feel the icy chilliness from the cool linoleum floor through my tights. My dot was in-between two boys that I had never met before. They talked lively to each other and sat somewhat too close to me, so that our crossed legs would touch. I therefore stretched out my legs instead, which caused the boys

> to immediately fill out the vacant space with their legs. . . . 'You're not sitting on your dot', I told the boy to my right. 'Can you move onto your dot, please?' The boy mocked me as the teacher told me to be quiet. . . . The teacher simply laughed lightly at what had happened. Then she said something about how difficult it was to learn how to sit still—especially for boys this age—but, she explained, that this was exactly what preschool was all about: learning how to sit still on your dot. (p. 2)

The dot on the cold floor is a performative agent in this story, implicated in producing a certain notion of learners and part of the context that contributes to the normalization of gendered bodies, in learning how to "act like a lady," as well as the dominant understanding that the point of early schooling is to get children to sit still.

Barad (2007) wrote that "matter and meaning are mutually articulated" (p. 152). She referred to practices as being both material and discursive at the same time. Looking at the material-discursive practices of schools involves asking research questions about both discursive norms and material arrangements, such as: What norms do teachers or parents bring to bear on interpreting their children's activities? How do the technologies they use shape their activities? How does the school's physical environment and the students' different neighborhoods impact and shape their relations? How do teachers' norms and interpretations produce notions of appropriateness? (Højgaard & Søndergaard, 2011). In contrast to typical research studies that try to distill causal relationships from the data, these questions are designed to recognize the complexities in processes of becoming and show how boundaries between subject positions, technologies, and physical spaces are entangled.

Doing research in third spaces involves investigating material-discursive practices while also understanding that research itself is an entangled material-discursive practice. Instead of assuming that there is a clear "I" conducting research—transparent and separate from the subjects of the research—researchers can use the idea of entanglement to recognize the inevitable ways the observer is inseparable from what is observed. Following Bohr's findings in the field of quantum physics that any act of observation changes the phenomenon being observed, changes will occur to both at once. The distinctions between "I" and the world, objective and subjective, the researcher and the researched, "become blurred when the field is moving you, the researcher, in unexpected directions and when the groupings of participants in the field encountered yesterday turn into something else the next day" (Tanggaard, 2013, p. 413). Given this entanglement, the role of the researcher needs to shift from the producer of knowledge to, what Tanggaard referred to as, the follower of traces. The researcher's role then is to look at ways of becoming and investigate the traces left behind by the activities of many actors in the course of unfolding events.

Researchers are unavoidably part of the instruments that transform whatever they observe or measure. "Conducting science in/by/with this world entails setting up apparatuses through which something can matter and thereby be studied. In a way," Juelskjær (2013) wrote, "one could say that it is about setting up fruitful experiments (i.e., research) in which the researcher is part of that very apparatus" (p. 756). Knowing and being are mutually implicated such that it is impossible to remove the researcher from their findings. "There is no such thing," Juelskjær said, "as 'knowing anything from a distance,' only knowing from within various and specific intra-actions" (p. 756).

Given the impossibility of studying anything from a distance, it makes little sense for educational research to be done exclusively by outside experts or consultants. Yet, recognizing that any observed phenomenon is changed by observation and by the observer does not mean that researchers must give up. It implies instead that teachers and students do their own research, not for the purpose of codifying best practices for pregiven outcomes but to reduce cultural invisibility and expand their perspectives and action possibilities.

References

Akom, A. A. (2009). Critical race theory meets participatory action research: Creating a community of Black youth as public intellectuals. In W. Ayers, T. M. Quinn, & D. Stovall (Eds.), *Handbook of social justice in education* (pp. 526–539). Routledge.

Bakhtin, M. (1981). *The dialogic imagination: Four essays*. University of Texas Press.

Ball, S. J. (1990). *Politics and policy making in education*. Routledge.

Barad, K. (2007). *Meeting the universe halfway: Quantum physics and the entanglement of matter and meaning*. Duke University Press.

Bell, D. (1987). *And we are not saved: The elusive quest for racial justice*. Basic Books.

Besley, A. C. (2003). Hybridized and globalized: Youth cultures in the postmodern era. *The Review of Education, Pedagogy, and Cultural Studies, 25*(2), 153–177.

Biesta, G. J. J. (2014). Pragmatising the curriculum: Bringing knowledge back into the curriculum conversation, but via pragmatism. *The Curriculum Journal, 25*(1), 29–49.

Blakely, E. (2007). *Interrupted narratives: Cultural invisibility in the classroom* [Unpublished master's thesis]. San Francisco State University.

Bourdieu, P. (1991). *Language and symbolic power.* Harvard University Press.

Brinkmann, S. (2013). *John Dewey: Science for a changing world.* Transaction Publishers.

Brown, J., Isaacs, D., & the World Café Community. (2005). *The World Café: Shaping our futures through conversations that matter.* Berrett-Koehler Publishers.

Canagarajah, A. S. (1996). From critical research practice to critical research reporting. *TESOL Quarterly, 30*(2), 321–331.

Coburn, C. E., & Penuel, W. R. (2016). Research–practice partnerships in education: Outcomes, dynamics, and open questions. *Educational Researcher, 45*(1), 48–54.

Coloma, R. S. (2009). "Destiny has thrown the Negro and the Filipino under the tutelage of America": Race and curriculum in the age of empire. *Curriculum Inquiry, 39*(4), 495–519.

Crenshaw, K. (1991). Mapping the margins: Intersectionality, identity politics, and violence against women of color. *Stanford Law Review, 43*(6), 1241–1299.

d'Agnese, V. (2017). The eclipse of imagination within educational 'official' framework and why it should be returned. *Studies in Philosophy in Education, 36*, 443–462.

Delgado, R., & Stefancic, J. (2017). *Critical race theory: An introduction* (Vol. 20). NYU Press.

Dewey, J. (1910). *How we think.* Cosimo Classics.

Dewey, J. (1925). *Experience and nature.* George Allen & Unwin.

Dewey, J. (1929). *The later works of John Dewey (1925–1953).* Southern Illinois University Press.

Dewey, J. (1934). *Art as experience.* Penguin Books.

Dewey, J. (1966). *Democracy and education.* The Free Press.

Dewey, J., Barnes, A. C., Buermeyer, L., Mullen, M., & De Mazia, V. (1947). *Art and education.* The Barnes Foundation Press.

Dixson, A. R., & Rousseau, C. K. (2005). And we still are not saved: Critical race theory in education ten years later. *Race Ethnicity and Education, 8*(1), 7–27.

Dreier, O. (2008). Learning in structures of social practice. In K. Nielsen, S. Brinkmann, C. Elmholdt, L. Tanggaard, P. Musaeus, & G. Kraft (Eds.), *A qualitative stance* (pp. 85–96). Aarhus University Press.

DuFour, R. (2004). What is a professional learning community? *Educational Leadership, 61*(8), 6–11.

Fals-Borda, O. (1987). The application of participatory action-research in Latin America. *International Sociology, 2*(4), 329–347.

Foucault, M. (1972). *The archaeology of knowledge and the discourse on language.* Pantheon Books.

Foucault, M. (1973). *The birth of the clinic: An archaeology of medical perception.* Vintage Books.

Foucault, M. (1977). *Discipline and punish: The birth of the prison.* Pantheon Books.

Foucault, M. (1990). *History of sexuality, Volumes 1–3.* Vintage Books.

Foucault, M. (2006). *History of madness.* Routledge.

Geertz, C. (1973). Deep play: Notes on the Balinese cockfight. *The interpretation of cultures* (pp. 412–453). Basic Books.

Greene, M. 1995. *Releasing the imagination: Essay on education, the arts, and social change.* Jossey-Bass.

Guo, S., Guo, Y., Beckett, G., Li, Q., & Guo, L. (2013). Changes in Chinese education under globalisation and market economy: Emerging issues and debates. *Compare, 43*(2), 244–264.

Hall, B. L. (2005). In from the cold? Reflections on participatory research from 1970–2005. *Convergence, 38*(1), 5–24.

Hall, G. S. (1931). *Adolescence—Its psychology and its relations to physiology, anthropology, sociology, sex, crime, and religion.* D. Appleton.

Hancock, A. M. (2007). When multiplication doesn't equal quick addition: Examining intersectionality as a research paradigm. *Perspectives on Politics, 5*(1), 63–79.

Hargreaves, A., & Shirley, D. L. (2009). *The fourth way: The inspiring future for educational change.* Corwin Press.

Heath, S. B. (1982). What no bedtime story means: Narrative skills at home and school. *Language in Society, 11*, 49–76.

Heath, S. B. (1983). *Ways with words: Language, life and work in communities and classrooms.* Cambridge University Press.

Holvino, E. (2008). Intersections: The simultaneity of race, gender and class in organization studies. *Gender, Work, and Organization, 17*(3), 248–277.

Holzkamp, K. (2013). *Psychology from the standpoint of the subject: Selected writings of Klaus Holzkamp.* Palgrave Macmillan.

Højgaard, L., & Søndergaard, D. M. (2011). Theorizing the complexities of discursive and material subjectivity: Agential realism and poststructural analyses. *Theory & Psychology, 21*(3), 338–354.

Juelskjær, M. (2013). Gendered subjectivities of spacetimematter. *Gender and Education, 25*(6), 754–768.

Khawaja, I., & Mørck, L. L. (2009). Researcher positioning: Muslim 'otherness' and beyond. *Qualitative Research in Psychology* 6(1–2), 28–45.

Kristensen, K-L., & Mørck, L. L. (2016). ADHD medication and social self-understanding: Social practice research with a first grade in a Danish primary school. *European Journal of Psychology of Education, 31*, 43–59.

Kuhn, T. S. (1969). *The structure of scientific revolutions.* University of Chicago Press.

Labov, W. (1972). *Language in the inner city: Studies in the Black English vernacular.* University of Pennsylvania Press.

Ladson-Billings, G., & Tate, W. F. (2016). Toward a critical race theory of education. In L. Parker & D. Gillborn (Eds.), *Critical race theory in education* (pp. 115–124). Routledge.

Lave, J. (2011). *Apprenticeship in critical ethnographic practice.* University of Chicago Press.

Lave, J. (2019). *Learning and everyday life: Access, participation, and changing practice.* Cambridge University Press.

Lenz Taguchi, H. (2010). *Going beyond the theory/practice divide in early childhood education: Introducing an intra-active pedagogy.* Routledge.

Lewis, C., Perry, R., & Murata, A. (2006). How should research contribute to instructional improvement? The case of lesson study. *Educational Researcher, 35*(3), 3–14.

Marzano, M. (2007). Informed consent, deception, and research freedom in qualitative research: A cross-cultural comparison. *Qualitative Inquiry, 13*(3), 417–436.

Mørck, L. L. (2010). Expansive learning as production of community. *Yearbook of the National Society for the Study of Education, 109*(1), 176–191.

Mørck, L. L. (2011). Studying empowerment in a socially and ethnically diverse social work community in Copenhagen, Denmark. *Ethos: Journal of the Society for Psychological Anthropology, 39*(1), 115–137.

Mørck, L. L., & Huniche, L. (2006). Critical psychology in a Danish context. *Annual Review of Critical Psychology (Online), 5*, 1–19.

Nielsen, K. (2006). Learning to do with things: Apprenticeship learning in bakery as economy and social practice. In A. Costall & O. Dreier (Ed.), *Doing things with things* (pp. 209–224). Ashgate Publishing.

Nielsen, K. (2009). A collaborative perspective on learning transfer. *Journal of Workplace Learning, 21*(1), 58–70.

Pérez Huber, L. (2020). *Moving beyond ethicality: Humanizing research methodologies with undocumented students and communities* (UCLA UndocuScholars' Policy and Research Brief Series). UCLA.

Rogoff, B. (2003). Thinking with the tools and institutions of culture. *The cultural nature of human development*. Oxford University Press.

Rorty, R. (1991). *Objectivity, relativism, and truth: Philosophical papers*. Cambridge University Press.

Rosaldo, R. (1989). *Culture and truth: The remaking of social analysis*. Beacon Press.

Sahlberg, P. (2007). Education policies for raising student learning: The Finnish approach. *Journal of Educational Policy, 22*(2), 147–171.

Sahlberg, P. (2011). The professional educator: Lessons from Finland. *American Educator, 35*(2), 34–38.

Solórzano, D., & Delgado Bernal, D. (2001). Critical race theory, transformational resistance and social justice: Chicana and Chicano students in an urban context. *Urban Education, 36*(3), 308–342.

Sue, D. W. (2004). Whiteness and ethnic monoculturalism: Making the "invisible" visible. *American Psychologist, 59*(8), 761–769.

Tanggaard, L. (2013). Troubling methods in qualitative inquiry and beyond. *Europe's Journal of Psychology, 9*(3), 409–418.

Torre, M., & Fine, M. (2006). Researching and resisting: Democratic policy research by and for youth. In S. Ginwright, P. Noguera, & J. Cammarota (Eds.), *Beyond resistance: Youth activism and community change* (pp. 269–286). Routledge.

Tuhiwai Smith, L. (1999). *Decolonizing methodologies: Research and indigenous peoples*. Zed Books.

Weems, L. (2004). Troubling professionalism: Narratives of family, race, and nation in educational reform. In B. M. Baker & K. E. Heyning (Eds.), *Dangerous coagulations?: The uses of Foucault in the study of education* (pp. 225–260). Peter Lang.

Willis, P. (2000). *The ethnographic imagination*. Polity Press.

Wolcott, H. F (1973). *The man in the principal's office: An ethnography*. Holt, Rinehart, & Winston.

Yosso, T. J. (2005). Whose culture has capital? A critical race theory discussion of community cultural wealth. *Race Ethnicity and Education, 8*(1), 69–91.

Yosso, T., Smith, W., Ceja, M., & Solórzano, D. (2009). Critical race theory, racial microaggressions, and campus racial climate for Latina/o undergraduates. *Harvard Educational Review, 79*(4), 659–691.

Conclusions

THERE IS COSTLY HUBRIS IN the field of education when research advisors, institutional review boards (IRBs), and funders insist that technocratic methods are the only valid approach to research. Despite widespread belief in their superiority, technocratic methods have not helped schools thrive or reduce historical inequities. The usual response to this failure is simply that "more research is needed." Repeating the same methods, however, is unlikely to produce different results.

The enforced technocratic paradigm limits the kinds of research that are possible and maintains the status quo. Flawed epistemologies, lack of funding, tight timelines, and narrow definitions of what constitutes "acceptable" research mean that graduate students and researchers must opt to perform simplistic quantitative studies with narrow variables, existing instrumentation, and predictable findings. They are often prohibited from studying the topics that matter to them and their communities.

The technocratic paradigm also alienates students. Universities ignore the fact that most students dread research methods courses and resist the high price of methods textbooks, which students find useful—if at all—only for passing exams and writing IRB proposals. There is no justification for the high price of these texts, as there is little difference in content among the widely available methods texts and the minimally revised editions that are reissued every few years to generate profits.

Alienating research methods courses are based on the banking style of education (Freire, 1970), in which students are expected to accept the content without question. Students are occasionally asked to critique the methodology of past studies but rarely, if ever, to critique the nature of technocratic methods or their underlying paradigms. Nor do they apply in class the data collection and analysis techniques they learn. They are prohibited from analyzing data from their own schools, since the methods course precedes the IRB approval process. Research methods content is thus decontextualized and made irrelevant.

Despite how the technocratic paradigm limits possibilities for doing relevant research, causes student alienation, and shows no capacity to reduce inequities, most professors, administrators, and policymakers persist in adhering to the paradigm. One reason for resisting change is that faculty identities are entangled with technocratic perspectives: Professors have been socialized into the paradigm in their doctoral studies, and they navigate a publish-or-perish system that rewards with funding and promotions their fidelity to the paradigm. If they critique technocratic norms, professors face institutional pressure from IRBs, funders, and promotion committees that endanger their chances to conduct research.

At the institutional level, universities, too, are tied to the technocratic paradigm. Major sources of research funding require using "rigorous" quantitative designs, and prestigious journals follow suit. There are only occasional nods toward alternative paradigms via marginalized mixed methods designs. Even programs and journals devoted to qualitative research retain an unexamined, underlying technocratic paradigm as they pursue "valid and reliable" studies.

There are many barriers to overcome before educators can develop their own inquiry practices. Professors, administrators, and policymakers believe that teachers cannot be trusted to perform research on their own classrooms, solve their own problems through inquiry, or reflect on their practice. The teaching profession has long been feminized, patronized, and deprofessionalized, and historically, educators have not controlled their own profession in the ways that lawyers, doctors, engineers, and other professionals do.

Given this context and continuing shortfalls in funding and support for education, it may be hard to imagine that practicing educators could pursue the kinds of inquiry practices discussed in this book. Yet the idea of teacher-driven inquiry is not far-fetched. Educators in some countries do have support to conduct their own research, including provision of planning and professional development time each day. This time is built into the schedule and does not require substitutes, nor does it mean a loss of consistent instructional time for students. In countries such as Finland, Singapore, Korea, and Hong Kong, teaching is a sought-after, highly respected, and well-paid career (Barber & Mourshed, 2007; Darling-Hammond, 2015; Low et al., 2011). Teacher preparation programs collaborate closely with local school systems, and teacher candidates are funded during preparation programs—instead of incurring debt and working for free. Teacher preparation, too, involves doing research. Teachers then enter schools as respected professionals who control their own profession and conduct their own practical inquiries.

The idea of taking on their own research may have little initial appeal for current teachers in the United States, who already feel overburdened. Underfunding means that it is rare for teachers to have sufficient planning time, much less the time for inquiry. Schools have insufficient professional staff, and teachers are left to fill the gaps. In many nations, by contrast, schools employ full-time school nurses, counselors, and other professionals to support students and enable teachers to conduct inquiry. The resource scarcity faced by many educators in the United States is not a forgone conclusion; it is a political choice.

Dismantling the historic inequities that schools produce requires a different choice. It means rejecting current research methods curricula and standardized testing regimes that reflect a technocratic research paradigm and neoliberal educational policies. It entails giving up the aimless bureaucratic tasks associated with articulating and evaluating SLOs. It requires rejecting the narrative of progress, which assumes that ever more technocratic research will generate best practices. It involves investing in teacher preparation programs and collaborative, democratic professional structures so that teachers can develop intelligent habits and expand third spaces for inquiry. It demands reconceptualizing learning so that students do not spend their days satisficing or being disciplined to sit still, but instead become full participants in communities that matter to them.

References

Barber, M., & Mourshed, M. (2007). *How the world's best-performing school systems come out on top*. McKinsey and Co.

Darling-Hammond, L. (2015). *The flat world and education: How America's commitment to equity will determine our future*. Teachers College Press.

Freire, P. (1970). *Pedagogy of the oppressed*. Continuum.

Low, E. L., Joseph, J., Atienza, J., Chng, S., Hui, C., & Lam, A. (Eds.). (2011). *Paving the fourth way: The Singapore story*. National Institute of Education.

Author Biographies

Erin Blakely graduated with a B.A. from the University of Michigan before moving to New York and working at an independent school for elementary and middle school students with learning differences. She earned her master's degree in education at San Francisco State University, where she later taught research methodologies in the Graduate College of Education. For her thesis, she conducted an ethnography on the normalization of narrative form in a diasporic community in Northern California. She spent the next decade coordinating action research projects, designing family leadership and English Language Learning programs for PreK-8 public schools, and facilitating county-wide equity initiatives. She subsequently did postgraduate work in Denmark. Her research interests include critical theory, cultural studies, pragmatism, social practice theory, history of the family, language socialization, narrative, and research design. She now lives in Southern California, working in higher education, writing, and making mixed media collages.

David Hemphill is Professor Emeritus in the Graduate College of Education at San Francisco State University, having worked there as a faculty member for more than 35 years. His research and teaching interests include international and multicultural education, cultural studies, critical theory, postmodern and postcolonial theory, popular culture and popular music, adult education, literacy, second language acquisition, and research methods. He received the Imogene Okes Research Award of the American Association for Adult, Alternative and Continuing Education for his adult literacy research. While at the university he led the development of two doctoral programs; pioneered multiple international initiatives; worked as a visiting scholar in Poland, Thailand, and Japan; and served as Department Chair, Director of Graduate Studies, and Associate Dean. Prior to coming to the university, Hemphill worked for a decade as an English language teacher and program director in community-based organizations in Oakland and San Francisco serving adult Asian immigrants and refugees. He holds a B.A. in political science and Asian languages from the University of California, Berkeley, and an M.A. in bilingual education and Ed.D. in educational organization and leadership from the University of San Francisco. He was brought up in Tokyo and Washington, DC, and he speaks several Asian and European languages. He is also a trombonist and musical arranger.

Index